(Painting by Jean-Léon Gérôme, Art Museum, Princeton University)

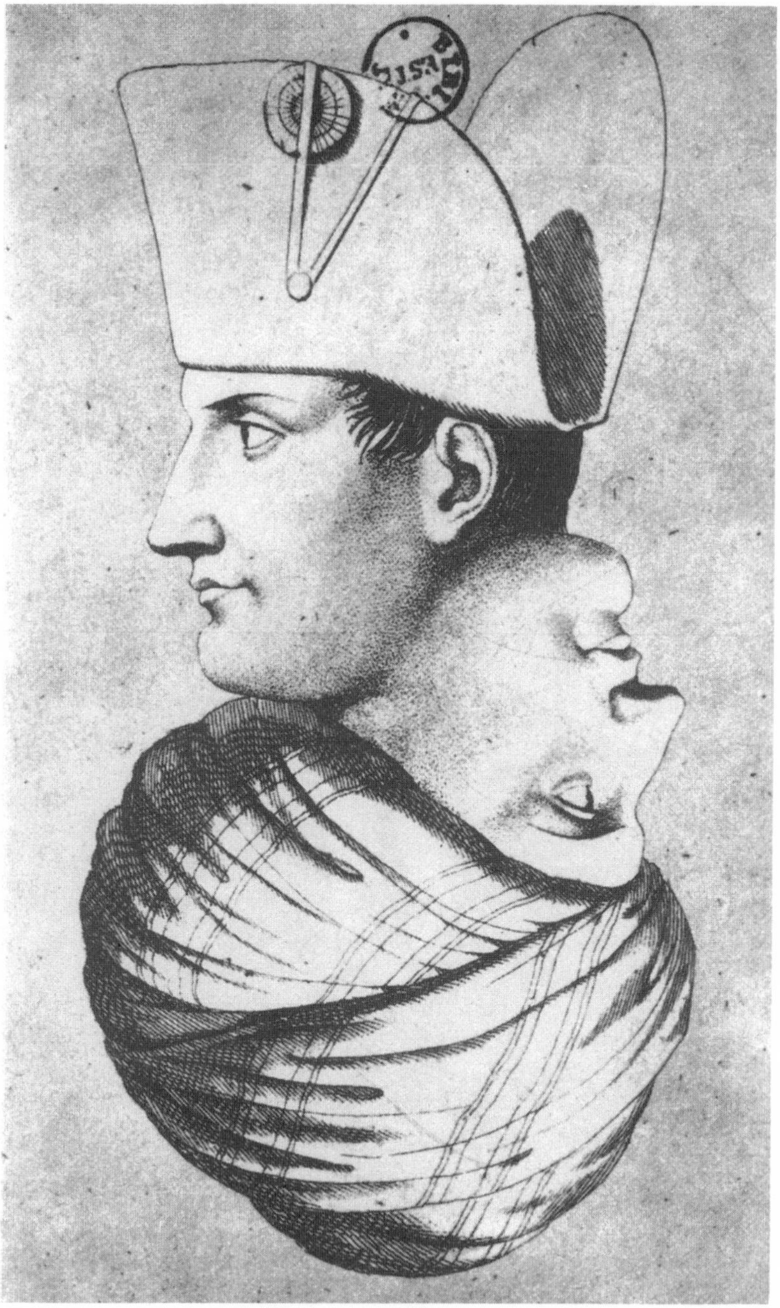

Double profile of Bonaparte with French bicorne army hat and turban
(Bibliothèque Nationale—Cabinet des Estampes)

Napoleon in Egypt

AL-JABARTĪ'S CHRONICLE OF THE FRENCH OCCUPATION, 1798

Introduction by
Robert L. Tignor

Translation by
Shmuel Moreh

Markus Wiener Publishers
Princeton

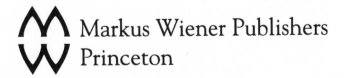

Fourth Printing 2001

For information write to: Markus Wiener Publishing, Inc.
231 Nassau Street, Princeton, NJ 08542

Library of Congress Cataloging-in-Publication Data

Jabartī, 'Abd al-Rahman, 1754-1822.
[Tarikh muddat al-Faransis bi-Misr. English]
Napoleon in Egypt: Al-Jabartī's chronicle of the first seven months of the French occupation of Egypt, 1798/translation by Shmuel Moreh;
introduction by Robert L. Tignor
ISBN 1-55876-069-5 ISBN 1-55876-070-9 (pbk.)
1. Napoleonic Wars, 1800-1815—Campaigns—Egypt.
2. Egypt—History—French occupation, 1798-1801. 3. Napoleon I, Emperor of the French, 1769-1821—Military leadership. 4. French—Egypt—History—19th century. I. Bourriene, Louis Antoine Fauvelet de, 1769-1834. Memoirs of Napoleon Bonaparte. 1993.
II. Said, Edward W., Scope of orientalism. 1993. III. Title.
DC225.J3413 1993 92-45614
940.2'7—dc20 CIP

The photographs in the text are reproduced courtesy of the following sources: page i, The Art Museum, Princeton University. Museum purchase, John Maclean Magie and Gertrude Magie Fund; All other pictures, Firestone Library, Princeton University.

Book Design by Cheryl Mirkin
This book has been composed in Goudy Old Style
by Coghill Book Typesetting Company, Richmond, Virginia

Printed in The United States of America on acid-free paper

CONTENTS

INTRODUCTION
BY ROBERT L. TIGNOR

On May 19, 1798, a massive French fleet set sail from Toulon harbor, bound for Egypt. Joined by smaller contingents from three other ports along the way, the fleet numbered 400 ships and transported 36,000 men. Under the command of France's rising new military officer, Napoleon Bonaparte, only 28 years old but already the most important military leader of the French revolution, the armada appeared off the coast of Alexandria on June 28th. An eyewitness, Nicholas the Turk, claimed that when the people looked at the water they could see only sky and ships and "were seized by unimaginable terror."

The French invasion of Egypt lasted for a brief three years (1798–1801) but constituted a watershed encounter between two civilizations. Though not as dramatic as Columbus's arrival in the New World or Cortés's conquest of Mexico, where a completely isolated segment of the world was brought into contact with Europe, the collision of cultural and political forces was nonetheless impressive. To be sure, Europe and the Muslim East had been in contact since the emergence of Islam in the seventh century. Even at the time of the invasion fifty or sixty French merchants resided in Egypt, and France had posted consular representatives to that country for the purpose of fostering trade. Yet the Egyptian population, in contrast to their Ottoman Turkish suzerains, had only the most rudimentary knowledge of European affairs. The intelligentsia and the ruling elite were largely unaware of the revolutionary events which had determined the French to invade Egypt. For them, then, the encounter with Bonaparte produced startling revelations, not the least of which was that Europe possessed superior military power, sufficient to defeat the vaunted Mamluk military machine, and that an expansionist, imperial, and cultural zeal drove France to possess the valley of the Nile.

The French invaders left the world the most copious records of their conquest of Ottoman Egypt—records which scholars have mined for the histories of the two countries in this period. The most impressive historical

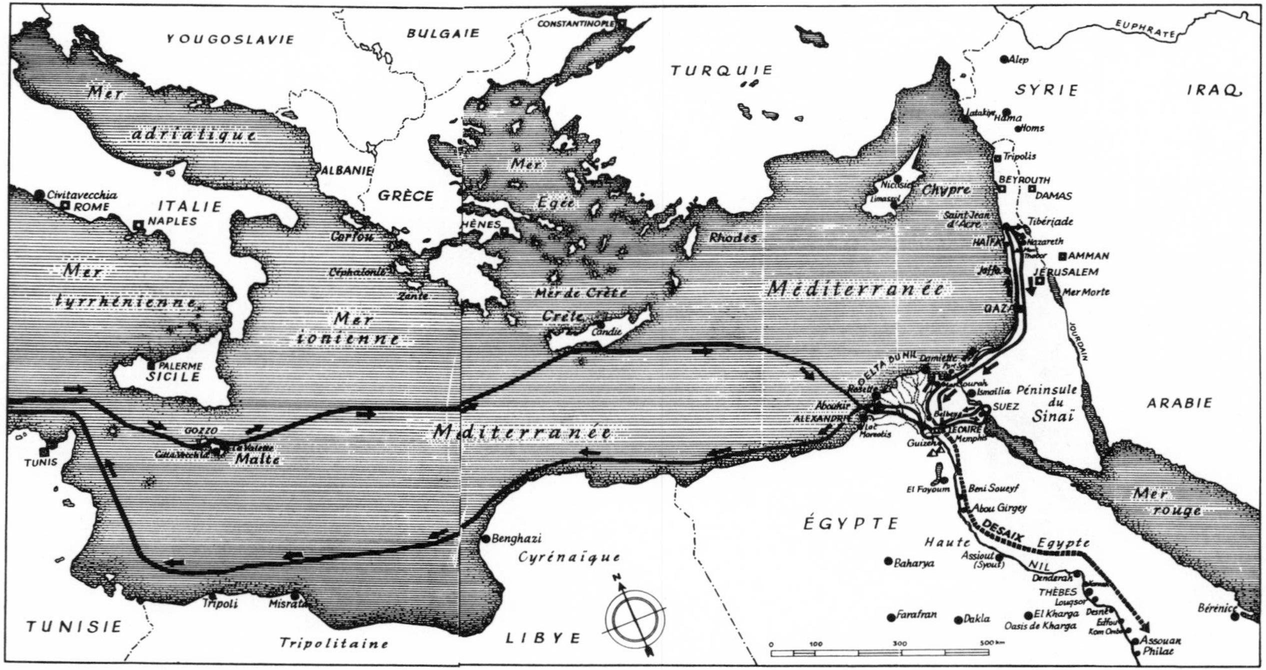

Bonaparte's route to and from Egypt

document to come out of the French occupation was the multi-volume *Description de l'Egypte*, which was the handiwork of the large contingent of scholars whom Napoleon had recruited for his conquest and colonization of Egypt.

Often the voices of the invaded are silent. We look in vain for their reactions to the trauma of invasion and occupation. African perceptions of the conquest of the African continent at the end of the nineteenth century would have gone unnoted save for the diligence of later researchers in recording African oral testimony. The Spanish conquest of the Americas in the sixteenth century left only sparse Indian records, in large measure because of the catastrophic loss of Indian life and the systematic destruction of Amerindian culture by Spanish overlords. Fortunately, the French occupation of Egypt produced no such effacement of indigenous accounts. The most important of the Egyptian observations were those set down by Egypt's unrivalled chronicler of the eighteenth century, Abd al-Rahman al-Jabartī.

In all, Jabartī wrote three versions of these cataclysmic years. His first work, entitled *Tārīkh muddat al-Faransīs bi Miṣr* and available in translation here, covers only a little more than six months of the French invasion. It offers Jabartī's immediate, often highly emotional responses, to the early days of French rule. It expresses the author's cynicism toward Napoleon's efforts to curry favor with the local population by claiming to be sympathetic to Islam while at the same time it reveals much admiration for French learning. Jabartī's second account, *Maẓhar al-taqdīs bi-zawāl dawlat al-Faransis,* would appear to have been written to put the author in the good graces of the Muslim rulers contending for power in the wake of the French withdrawal. It rejected the French occupation in all of its manifestations. The final study, the famous *Ajā'ib al-āthar fil-tarājim wal-Akhbar,* chronicled the history of Egypt from 1688 until 1821. A portion of this work presented, in a dispassionate tone, the events of the French occupation.

We know little of the life of Ottoman Egypt's most illustrious historian, save that he was born into a family of *ulama* (religious scholars) in 1753 and died in 1825 or 1826. His most important work, *Ajā ib,* was long forbidden publication because of its many criticisms of Muhammad Ali, Viceroy of Egypt from 1805 until 1849 and founder of Egypt's ruling dynasty. Only at the end of 1870 was the ban on its publication lifted, and only in 1879–80 was the entire work published.

The *Muddat* commences in the middle of June, 1798, with news of the arrival of a British fleet under the command of Horatio Nelson off the coast of Alexandria. Nelson had come in search of the French fleet under Napo-

Visit to the Pyramids of Gizeh

leon, and the two fleets had passed in the night without encountering each other. The account leaves off in December, 1798, with Napoleon still trying to secure his hold over a recalcitrant Egyptian population. Although it deals with only a brief period in the French occupation, it treats all of the most important themes of French rule, including the military clash with the Mamluks, the French efforts to organize a settled and collaborative government in Egypt, and the first and most aggressive uprising of the Cairene population against the French. It also presents, admittedly from the perspective of the author, the attitude of local inhabitants toward the French colonizers.

The decision to occupy Egypt did not spring full-blown from the fertile brain of Napoleon Bonaparte. France's economic interests in Egypt were rising in the eighteenth century, by the end of which Egypt was France's leading trading partner, outside of the sugar islands of the Caribbean. French diplomats had proposed several schemes for conquering and colonizing Egypt well before the French revolution. It fell to Napoleon, however, to put these ideas into practice. This he did with the flair and comprehensiveness for which he was already well known. Following his expulsion of the British from Toulon, his suppression of a Parisian royalist uprising against the Convention, and his military triumphs in North Italy in 1796, the French Directory named him to command the Army of England. Although this army was ostensibly intended to conquer England, Napoleon realized the folly of such an effort, given the British command of the seas. He proposed, instead, to strike at British interests in India and throughout Asia by invading Egypt. Having secured the assent of the Directory, he assembled an armada and a powerful army of occupation. Nor did he neglect the cultural aspects of the undertaking. The French revolution had propelled an arsenal of new political, cultural, and social ideals into world history. In selecting a group of scientists to aid the colonization effort, Napoleon chose leading men of science who in addition to their technical skills were suffused with the ideals of the French revolution.

In 1798 Egypt was still formally part of the Ottoman empire. In reality, Mamluk military households ruled the country. Ottoman forces had conquered Egypt in 1517 and incorporated it as a prized possession. The Ottomans continued to exercise suzerainty over the country in the eighteenth century. They appointed a political representative to the country and received annual tribute payments. But Ottoman political and military influence was waning. The seven Ottoman military corps, including the feared Janissaries, or military slaves recruited from Christian families in the Balkans, had yielded military supremacy to the Mamluks.

Exactly when the Mamluks established political supremacy in Ottoman Egypt is not clear. These military households increased their numbers by taking young boys away from their parents, introducing them into Mamluk households as slave recruits, and preparing them for political and military service. These slave levies were drawn at first overwhelmingly from the Caucasus but later from the Sudan and other parts of Africa as well. As Jabartī's account indicates, the Mamluks were not the only influential group. Through ties of wealth they had aligned themselves with merchant and *ulama* groups. Egypt's ruling elite constituted a tiny fraction of the total population. The vast majority were peasants and artisans who had little say in governance and were viewed by their rulers mainly as taxpayers.

Napoleon's military defeat of the Mamluk forces, just outside Cairo, at the so-called battle of the pyramids, sent shock waves throughout the Muslim

East. The French force had the advantage of numbers—25,000 against a probable 15,000. But the Mamluk profession was warfare. As they marched out to meet the French, one of their princes boasted: "Let the Franks come; we shall crush them beneath our horses' hooves." The Mamluk warriors were, if nothing else, a spectacle to behold. Their elaborate and resplendent military regalia was intended to evoke fear in their adversaries. Literally armed to the teeth, they carried javelins, sabers, battle axes, bows, and muskets and were surrounded by a retinue of followers whose function was to assist rather than to fight. Nonetheless, they proved no match for the superior weaponry, advanced military tactics, and determination of the French forces. By the time the battle ended, the Mamluk forces were in disarray. Egypt's two rulers, Ibrahim Bey and Murad Bey, had fled. Ibrahim had retreated to Syria and Murad to Upper Egypt. Shortly after the conflict, the French entered Cairo, and Napoleon installed himself in the house of a local notable, Muhammad Bey al-Alfi.

From the outset Napoleon intended to colonize Egypt. To do so he sought the support of the local population. As a first step he issued a proclamation, contained in Jabartī's account. Asserting that the French had entered the country not to destroy Islam but to liberate its inhabitants from Mamluk tyranny, Napoleon hoped to align himself with Egypt's merchants, *ulama*, and lesser notables. The proclamation also made clear, as did subsequent French actions, that resistance to French authority would be met with stern reprisals. Napoleon followed his proclamation by creating local governing councils, *diwans*, which, while advisory and subordinate to French military commanders, had local Egyptian representation. The first *diwan* was established in Cairo. Additional councils were set up in each of the sixteen administrative districts into which the French divided Egypt. Later, Napoleon created a grand *diwan*, which drew representatives from all of Egypt's districts as well as Cairo and which selected Shaykh al-Sharqawi as its President.

The invasion and the efforts of the French to create a settled administration in Egypt provoked determined opposition among the local population. The French task was rendered even more difficult when the Ottoman Sultan proclaimed a holy war and called upon the local inhabitants to rise against the occupiers. Jabartī's account suggests that a number of oppressive French policies alienated the Egyptian population and deepened the antagonism against the occupying force. French military and administrative plans were costly. The new rulers were compelled to place heavy tax demands on the people. They also forced merchants to advance them funds, and they confiscated the property of the Mamluks as well as properties for which Egyptian claimants failed to produce adequate records.

Jabartī's account of the October 21–22 Cairo uprising offers a valuable Egyptian perspective on these events. The *Muddat* leaves no doubt that *ulama*, like Jabartī himself, distrusted Napoleon's proclamations and rallied the people against the French. Using mosques as meeting places, the rebel leaders attacked the French for their fiscal policies but also pointed out the widespread French infringements of traditional rights and Islamic customs. Yet the rebellion failed. It was unable to win the support of all of Cairo but was confined to a few severely disaffected quarters where hot-headed recalcitrants filled the population with rumor and inaccurate information. The French response was quick and severe. Stationing their cannons on high ground and raining down fire on the most rebellious locations, including even the venerated al-Azhar mosque, the French brought the resistance to an end within 36 hours. Even after suppressing overt opposition, the French carried out further acts of punishment, including executions, against those individuals deemed responsible for inciting the rebellion or joining it.

The short-lived October 21–22 uprising proved a harbinger for future Franco-Egyptian relations. Although Jabartī recounts no further acts of opposition in the *Muddat*, in fact French forces were harassed during the remainder of their stay in Egypt.

At this point the narrative breaks off. The French were still attempting to complete their control of the country and had even embarked upon a campaign to conquer the holy places and Syria. There, in Syria, Napoleon suffered his first military reversal. At the city of Acre the French forces ground to a halt. Ottoman troops, the British fleet, and the ravages of disease wreaked havoc among the French forces and persuaded Napoleon to lead his army back to Egypt. By the time he reached the valley of the Nile he had lost 2,000 of the 13,000 who had embarked upon the campaign. Another 3,000 had suffered casualties.

No doubt Napoleon intended to fulfill his mission in Egypt and establish a full-fledged French presence there. But he kept an eye on events in France. By the middle of 1799 he realized that his army was by now trapped in Egypt. The British had destroyed the French fleet off Abukir on August 1, 1798, and the Ottomans had landed troops in Egypt to oppose the French. At home France had lost much territory to its adversaries. Determined to play a large role on France's political and military stage he left Egypt. Keeping his plans secret from all but a few trusted individuals, Napoleon stole away from Cairo on August 18, 1799, embarked from Alexandria on August 22,

Portrait of Kléber (Drawing by E. Charpentier)

and after 47 days at sea arrived back in France. Within three months of his departure from Egypt he had seized power in France. He established himself as the First Consul of the newly established Consulate government which had replaced the Directory. While thousands of his soldiers remained trapped in Egypt amid an increasingly hostile population and suffered greatly from disease, the young French general had set his course toward the mastery of Europe.

At his departure Napoleon placed Jean-Baptiste Kléber in command. He did not inform Kléber of this decision, no doubt because he knew of Kléber's growing hostility to the Egyptian venture and to his own handling of affairs there. Once in command Kléber sought but one goal—an agreement with his Ottoman and British adversaries by which he would be permitted to evacuate the Egyptian army to France. An agreement, struck on January 24, 1800, and initialed by the English naval commander, Sidney Smith, as well as the Ottomans, was repudiated in London. Unable to leave the country, Kléber turned his attention to securing dominion over Egypt. Even here he was frustrated, and on June 6 he was assassinated by a religious enthusiast from Aleppo. His successor was Jacques-Abdallah Menou, a man who had converted to Islam while in Egypt so that he could marry an Egyptian woman. Unable to maintain the French military position in Egypt, Menou had to accede to British surrender terms. On July 31, 1801, the French forces began to leave Egypt; the last soldier had departed by the end of September. The brief but important French occupation was brought to a close.

Modern scholarship regards the French invasion and occupation of Egypt as opening the modern era in the Arab world. The French forces, the argument runs, exposed the military weaknesses of the region and awakened the educated classes to the learning of the West. To be sure, an occupation lasting a mere three years could not produce far-reaching and fundamental institutional and intellectual changes. Yet by defeating the Mamluk cavalry and sowing confusion among the ruling elements in Egypt the French occupation set in motion a train of events which changed the face of Egypt and the rest of the Middle East. In Egypt itself, an Albanian military adventurer, Muhammad Ali, took advantage of the power vacuum created by the defeat of the Mamluks and the withdrawal of the French. Triumphing over the Ottomans and the remnants of Mamluk military power, Muhammad Ali consolidated his authority in the Nile valley in 1805 and thereafter effected far-reaching, albeit autocratic changes in virtually every arena of Egyptian life. Not surprisingly, he drew freely upon France for technical advice. He

Bonaparte fleeing from Egypt back to France (Humorous engraving by Gillray)

encouraged French military and cultural leaders to create French-style institutions in Egypt and to assist in what proved to be the Middle East's most dramatic and successful effort at defensive modernization. The linkage between Muhammad Ali's reforms and the French invasion was clear. French successes in Egypt spurred the thinking of Muhammad Ali and his advisers who looked to France as the model European country for their development. In return French savants and military men, inspired by the almost mythic qualities of the Napoleonic stay in Egypt, gladly made their talents available to Egypt. The Franco-Egyptian alliance was propitious. In Muhammad Ali's Egypt Western education, new industrial projects, irrigation works, and cash-crop agriculture set the country on new pathways.

In preparation for the invasion Napoleon assembled a talented group of young scientists to accompany his forces to that country. Inspired by the ideals of the Enlightenment and eager to patronize learning, Napoleon took with him to Egypt more than 500 civilians, of whom 151 were members of the special Commission des Sciences et Arts. To lead the scientific contingent Napoleon chose two scientific luminaries—Gaspard Monge and Claude-Louis Berthollet, then in their fifties and well known for their impressive work in the fields of geometry and chemistry. Other men enrolled in the Commission included Jean-Baptiste-Joseph Fourier, just thirty years old and soon to be the inventor of the system of mathematical analysis which bears his name, Etienne Geoffroy Saint-Hilaire, a naturalist, Déodat de Dolomieu, a mineralogist, and the artist Vivant Denon. The great majority of the scientists were young men, recent graduates of the Ecole Polytechnique and the Ecole des Ponts et Chaussees. In Egypt they set up the Institute of Egypt, the workings of which Jabartī describes toward the end of his *Muddat.*

The monument to the energy of the Commission des Sciences et Arts was the *Description de l'Egypte,* published between 1809 and 1828 and containing ten albums of plates, 9 volumes of text, and three volumes of atlases and maps. The first five albums were devoted to the Egyptian antiquities and launched the field of Egyptology. Two additional albums dealt with Egypt in 1800. Along with the volumes of text they offered the most detailed depiction of a Middle Eastern society on the eve of the modern era. The final three albums illustrated the natural history of the Nile valley and Red Sea. So powerful was the Egyptian monumental architectural style as illustrated in the *Description* that it came to dominate the artistic sensibility of Napoleonic Europe.

Jabartī's account of his frequent meetings with the French savants at the Institute of Egypt and his astonishment at their learning demonstrate that at least a few Egyptian men of letters took an interest in French thought and were welcomed by the French scholars. Yet it is to be doubted that the influence of the French savants reverberated deeply throughout Egyptian society, even among the intelligentsia. French scientists were busy with practical assignments on behalf of the French military. They were meant to serve the interests of the French generals and not to fraternize with the Egyptian *ulama.*

Jabartī's *Muddat* contained no disquisitions about the meaning for Egypt and its people of revolutionary France. Jabartī did not analyze the French motives for being in Egypt or speculate on the challenge French arms and ideas posed to Egypt's future. At all times Jabartī was the careful chronicler, the recorder of events, rather than the analyzer. Yet the text hinted that the invasion created new challenges for Egyptian society. To begin with, Jabartī offered two explanations for the French military success. First, he praised the French forces for their skill and zeal and likened them to early Islamic conquerors engaged in holy war. Such high praise for the French betokened deep respect, even fear. In contrast, Jabartī scorned the Mamluk preparations and the terror and confusion which spread throughout the Egyptian population as they learned of the French advance on Cairo. Alexandria fell without resistance, according to Jabartī, because the Mamluks neglected its fortifications, fearing that they would be used by local opponents to undermine central Mamluk power.

The geometrician Fourier
(Drawing by Dutertre)

The French efforts to administer Egypt receive a mixed, though largely negative, evaluation. Jabartī was cynical of Napoleonic proclamations and excoriated the French leader for his irreligion. Bonaparte's attack on the Papal See, far from winning Jabartī's approval, only demonstrated to the Egyptian chronicler Napoleon's attitude toward all religions. Moreover, Jabartī disparaged the French effort to Arabize their propaganda and described the French writing in Arabic as vulgar and full of grammatical errors. He portrayed the French forces themselves, including Napoleon, whom Jabartī referred to throughout as *Sari Askar* (Commanding General), as rapacious. They were eager to lay their hands on people's property in illegitimate and deceitful ways. Yet Jabartī was intrigued with certain administrative innovations, not the least of which were the councils *(diwans)*, by which the French sought to place themselves in contact with Egyptian notables. In two separate places he described in considerable detail the elaborate procedures, including secret ballots and voice votes, by which these councils designated their presidents. Although he offered no comment on these procedures and what the French intended by them, it was apparent that Napoleon's attempt to introduce French bureaucratic practices awakened this man's interest.

Jabartī's account of the French invasion and occupation is one of the finest chronicles of a European encounter with a non-European people as told from the vantage point of the non-European. We are fortunate to have available an expert translation undertaken by the distinguished Israeli scholar and

Arabist, Shmuel Moreh, and we are pleased to make this work accessible to readers once again.

The French wrote numerous accounts of their experiences in Egypt. There have also been many scholarly treatments of this important moment in Franco-Egyptian history. Among the best of the French eyewitness observations are the memoirs of Antoine Fauvelet de Bourrienne, a schoolmate of Napoleon from their days at the military school at Brienne-le-Château in the early 1780s. Napoleon then employed Bourrienne as his private secretary beginning in 1797, and Bourrienne accompanied Napoleon on his campaign in Egypt. Although the two men had a falling out later in their careers and Bourrienne ceased to be Napoleon's private secretary and confidant, the memoirs, first published in 1829 and a popular sensation from the moment of their publication, make for interesting reading. They have been attacked for inaccuracies and for an animus against Napoleon, but the accounts selected for this book arose when Bourrienne was working along with Napoleon and have stood the test of time. According to Prince Metternich, commenting on the memoirs when they first appeared, they were "both interesting and amusing." Metternich went on to add that "they are the only authentic memoirs of Napoleon which have yet appeared. The style is not brilliant but that only makes them the more trustworthy." We have taken from this massive work those chapters which parallel the Jabartī account and time period.

The Napoleonic expedition marked a new era of more aggressive European relations toward the Middle East. Although the French and British were both compelled to withdraw their forces from Egypt, European-Ottoman relations had now swung decisively in favor of Europe. Foundations were being established for Europe's imperial sway in the Middle East. According to the eminent literary scholar Edward W. Said, the Napoleonic expedition crystallized deep-seated, long-held, and largely derogatory images which Europeans had of the Muslim world. We take pleasure in presenting Professor Said's stimulating discussion of the Napoleonic invasion and its impact on Western thought concerning the Orient in his important study, *Orientalism*.

Princeton
January 1993

AL-JABARTĪ'S CHRONICLE OF THE FIRST SEVEN MONTHS OF THE FRENCH OCCUPATION OF EGYPT, JUNE-DECEMBER 1798 MUḤARRAM-RAJAB 1213

TRANSLATED BY S. MOREH

Mourad Bey, head of the Mameluks
(Drawing by Dutertre in "Description de l'Egypte")

The Translated Text

This is the history of the period of the French in Egypt from the year [A.H.] *1213 until* [A.H.] *1216 by the most learned 'Abd al-Raḥmān al-Jabartī al-Miṣrī, in his own handwriting, may God have mercy on him.*

The year [A.H.] one thousand two hundred and thirteen [/A.D. 1798]

At the beginning of this year the Sultan of Islam was the Sultan Salīm ibn Muṣṭafā the Ottoman, and the Pasha of Egypt was Bakr Pasha, the Pasha of al-Shām was 'Abd Allāh Pasha ibn al-'Aḍm and Aḥmad Pasha al-Jazzār who had been dismissed[1] from al-Shām had fortified himself in Acre, the Grand Vizier was Muḥammad Pasha 'Izzat, the Amīrs of Egypt were Ibrāhīm Bey[2] and Murād Bey[3] and their Khushdāshs (comrades) who were Sulaymān Bey al-Aghā,[4] Ibrāhīm Bey al-Wālī,[5] 'Uthmān Bey al-Sharqāwī,[6] Ayyūb Bey al-Kabīr[7] (the elder), Ayyūb Bey al-Daftardār,[8] Aḥmad Bey al-Kilārjī,[9] Muṣṭafā Bey,[10] Ṣāliḥ Bey[11] Amīr of the Pilgrimage, and Qāsim Bey Abū Sayf.[12] The Ṣanjaqs of Ibrāhīm Bey were 'Uthmān Bey al-Ashqar,[13] Marzūq Bey[14] the son of Ibrāhīm Bey, 'Abd al-Raḥmān Bey,[15] Qāsim Bey al-Mūsquwā,[16] Qāsim Bey[17] Amīn al-Baḥrayn (the holder of the two ports, old Cairo and Būlāq), Murād Bey al-Ṣaghīr[18] (the younger), and Rashwān Bey.[19] The Ṣanjaqs of Murād Bey were Muḥammad Bey al-Alfī,[20] 'Uthmān Bey al-Jūkhadār,[21] 'Uthmān Bey al-Bardīsī,[22] Salīm Bey Abū 'l-Diyāb,[23] Muḥammad Bey al-Manfūkh,[24] their Amīrs and Kāshifs being too many to list. Moreover, each Kāshif had about fifty *mamlūks*. The deposed Ṣanjaqs were 'Uthmān Bey Ṭabl al-Ismā'īlī,[25] Muḥammad Bey al-Mabdūl,[26] Bīkīr Bey,[27] Muḥammad Bey Kishkish, Ḥasan Bey Qaṣaba Riḍwān, Zayn al-Fiqār Bey,[28] and others; as well as the rest of the government officials and the Ujāqs.[29]

Among this year's events: on Sunday the tenth of Muḥarram messengers arrived with letters bearing word that ten European ships had reached the port of Alexandria on Thursday the eighth, and had stopped at such a distance that the inhabitants of the port could see them. A short while later another fifteen ships had appeared. The inhabitants of the port had been awaiting their messenger when suddenly a caique came from these ships bearing ten men. When they reached the shore the people of the town spoke with them asking them who they were. They replied that they were English who had come to enquire about the French. The people of the town told them: 'No French are with us except those who reside in the port'. The English informed them that the French had set out from their country with a great fleet. They further said: 'We are their enemies and do not know in which direction they intend to sail. Perhaps they will attack you suddenly and you will not be able to repel them'. However, al-Sayyid Muḥammad Kurayyim did not believe their words and thought them to be trickery. The English thereupon requested: 'Sell us water and provisions according to their value and we shall stay in our ships lying in wait for them. When they come we shall take care of the matter and save you the trouble'. The above-mentioned Muḥammad Kurayyim declined their offer and said: 'We do not accept what you say nor will we give you anything'. Then he expelled them that God's will might be fulfilled.

Ten days had passed when suddenly the French came. Since the English had come to them, questioned them, and departed from their midst, anxiety and doubts had seized the people of the port, so they sent letters to the Kāshif of al-Buḥayra and the bedouin asking that they come and protect them. This letter [*sic*] was read out before the people and they discussed its [*sic*] contents among themselves.

On the third day more letters arrived with words that the ships were no longer visible so people calmed down and their prattlings ceased. As for the Amīrs, they neither cared nor bothered themselves with this matter.

On Wednesday, the twentieth of Muḥarram, news and letters arrived from the ports of Alexandria, Rosetta, and Damanhūr with word that on Monday the eighteenth, the people of the port suddenly realized that the French and their ships had reached al-'Ajamī, and were advancing on the town at daybreak[30] by land like a swarm of locusts. The people were excited and their shouts filled the air. Then the inhabitants of the port, the Kāshif of al-Buḥayra, and the bedouin who were with him attacked the French and fought them fiercely. As a result

Arrival of the French fleet off the Egyptian coast

a great number of the people of the port were killed and the rest fled. The Kāshif also fled and saved himself. Meanwhile the French continuously increased in number. They scaled the ruined parts of the wall surrounding the port and entered it. The people looked about and suddenly found the French behind them, and withdrew in haste seeking their homes only to discover that the French had occupied the new Manshiyya and had surrounded the walls. The people took refuge in the inns, khāns, and houses and locked themselves in. Others fortified themselves and locked themselves in the big tower and the Citadel, firing continuously for some time from the tops of the houses and windows with bullets, but their gunpowder ran out and they were not at all prepared. The Citadel and tower also were devoid of ammunition. Furthermore they saw / the fire coming at them from every side so they asked for safe-conduct (*amān*) and were granted it. Then the French stopped the fighting and proclaimed safe-conduct. Soon afterwards, the notables of the town went out to the French who received them. Then they raised their flags which are known among them as *bandīrāt* (*bandiera*), disarmed the populace, and had them sew their emblem (*cocarde*) on their breasts. Furthermore the French levied impost for the upkeep of the military (*kulaf*) and demanded money.

When the news of these events reached Cairo, alarm took hold of the populace. Ibrāhīm Bey thereupon set out on horseback to Qaṣr al-'Aynī where he met with Murād Bey, the Amīrs, the Qāḍī, and the Shaykhs who came to him, and together they discussed these events. One of the Shaykhs said: 'All this is a result of negligence in managing the ports and letting things slide, to such a degree that the enemy could occupy the port of Islam'. Murād Bey exclaimed: 'What can we do, for whenever we want to rebuild and fortify you claim: "their intention is rebellion against the Sultan", and this is what has prevented us from acting'. Such were their excuses, as frail as a spider's web,[31] for since the time of 'Alī Bey not only did they not pay sufficient attention to the port but even removed what weapons and cannons were already there! Furthermore they stopped the flow of the salaries (*murattabāt*) due to the garrisons (*murābiṭīn*), and soldiers stationed (*al-'askar al-mutaqayyidīn*) at the port, took their wages (*'alūfāt*) and cut off their revenues (*'awāyid*). As for the weapons, nothing remained except some broken-down cannons which were useless. It happened once that they needed gunpowder to fire the cannon on the Feast but they could not even find enough to load it once so they had to buy powder from the druggist. All this after Alexandria and its towers had once been extremely well built and fortified with an excellent wall surrounding her; a wall which had been maintained by former generations. Three hundred and sixty towers were incorporated into this wall, corresponding to the days of the year. Every tower had its own ammunition depot, supplies, and garrison. All these were neglected until nothing remained while the wall and its towers fell into ruin, until in some places the walls became level with the ground.

Then they agreed to write a report about what had happened and send it to the government (in Constantinople). They wrote it and the Pasha sent it with his own messenger by land. They believed that the ailing or sick man who had been bitten by a snake would remain in his present state until the antidote would arrive from Iraq.[32]

Finally they agreed that an army should set out against the French with Murād Bey as Ṣārī 'Askar (commander-in-chief). People were saying that the moment that Murād Bey arrived at his destination, victory would be theirs. At this point they hastily started preparing and organizing themselves and soon found that they had few supplies so they began to raid the storehouses for water-skins and other things.

On Friday after prayer Murād Bey set out on horseback to al-Jisr al-Aswad and stayed there for two days until his troops, his Amīrs, and Ṣanjaqs had all arrived. Accompanying Murād Bey were 'Alī Pasha al-Ṭarābulsī and Naṣūḥ Pasha.

He took a great number of cannons, grenades, and bombs with him as well as a store of gunpowder and cannon balls. In addition a great number of galleon-men and cannoneers set out with Murād Bey's army together with several ships, sea soldiers, and small galleons[33] which he had built. He had built seven galleons, three of which were large ones, imitating the Sultan, and had spent enormous sums of money upon them. He had also manned them with troops and sailors, providing them with supplies and high pay. He had them stationed in front of his palace at Jīza for a long time as decoration to glorify himself before his own people and others. The big galleons which the water could not carry he left behind, and took the small ones, the dhahabiyyas,[34] the qanjas,[35] and ghurābs.[36] Upon reaching al-Jisr al-Aswad he sent to Cairo ordering that an iron chain of great thickness and strength should be made, of a length of one hundred and thirty cubits. He ordered that this chain should be set up at the inlet of Rosetta at the two towers of Mughayzal, stretching from bank to bank so that the French ships would be prevented from passing into the Nile, this being on the advice of 'Alī Pasha. In addition he commanded that a bridge of boats with barricades and cannons should be erected, on the assumption that the French would not dare to advance rapidly or at least that they could hold them off and endure until they would be able to carry out their plans.

During the course of these events gloom spread among the populace and was felt in the market-places and people withdrew / to their homes from sunset onward. As a result the Aghā and the Wālī publicly called for the reopening of the markets and the coffee-houses and ordered that lamps outside the houses and shops be lit once again. This was done for two reasons: firstly, to dispel the gloom and create an atmosphere of ease and comfort and secondly, out of fear that an alien might have free rein in the town.

On Monday news arrived that the French had reached Damanhūr and Rosetta, bringing about the flight of their inhabitants to Fuwwa and its surroundings. Contained in this news was mention of the French sending notices throughout the country demanding impost for the upkeep of the military. Furthermore they printed a large proclamation in Arabic, calling on the people to obey them and to raise their 'Bandiera'. In this proclamation were inducements, warnings, all manner of wiliness and stipulations. Some copies were sent from the provinces to Cairo and its text is:[37]

In the name of God, the Merciful, the Compassionate. There is no god but God. He has no son, nor has He an associate in His Dominion.

On behalf of the French Republic which is based upon the foundation of liberty and equality, General Bonaparté, Commander-in-Chief of the French armies makes known to all the Egyptian people that for a long time the Ṣanjaqs who lorded it over Egypt have treated the French community basely and contemptuously and have persecuted its merchants with all manner of extortion and violence. Therefore the hour of punishment has now come.

Unfortunately this group of Mamlūks, imported from the mountains of Circassia and Georgia have acted corruptly for ages in the fairest land that is to be found upon the face of the globe. However, the Lord of the Universe, the Almighty, has decreed the end of their power

O ye Egyptians, they may say to you that I have not made an expedition hither for any other object than that of abolishing your religion; but this is a pure falsehood and you must not give credit to it, but tell the slanderers that I have not come to you except for the purpose of

Bey Mameluk (Lithography by Carle Vernet)

restoring your rights from the hands of the oppressors and that I more than the Mamlūks, serve God — may He be praised and exalted — and revere His Prophet Muḥammad and the glorious Qur'ān.

And tell them also that all people are equal in the eyes of God and the only circumstances which distinguish one from the other are reason, virtue, and knowledge. But amongst the Mamlūks, what is there of reason, virtue, and knowledge, which would distinguish them from others and qualify them alone to possess everything which sweetens life in this world? Wherever fertile land is found it is appropriated to the Mamlūks; and the handsomest female slaves, and the best horses, and the most desirable dwelling-places, all these belong to them exclusively. If the land of Egypt is a fief of the Mamlūks, let them then produce the title-deed, which God conferred upon them. But the Lord of the Universe is compassionate and equitable toward mankind, and with the help of the Exalted, from this day forward no Egyptian shall be excluded from admission to eminent positions nor from acquiring high ranks, therefore the intelligent and virtuous and learned (*'ulamā'*) amongst them, will regulate / their affairs, and thus the state of the whole population will be rightly adjusted.

Formerly, in the lands of Egypt there were great cities, and wide canals and extensive commerce and nothing ruined all this but the avarice and the tyranny of the Mamlūks.

O ye Qāḍīs, Shaykhs and Imāms; O ye Shurbājiyya and men of circumstance tell your nation that the French are also faithful Muslims, and in confirmation of this they invaded Rome and destroyed there the Papal See, which was always exhorting the Christians to make war with Islam. And then they went to the island of Malta, from where they expelled the Knights, who claimed that God the Exalted required them to fight the Muslims. Furthermore, the French at all times have declared themselves to be the most sincere friends of the Ottoman Sultan and the enemy of his enemies, may God ever perpetuate his empire! And on the contrary the Mamlūks have withheld their obeisance from the Sultan, and have not followed his orders. Indeed they never obeyed anything but their own greed!

Blessing on blessing to the Egyptians who will act in concert with us, without any delay, for their condition shall be rightly adjusted, and their rank raised. Blessing also, upon those who will abide in their habitations, not siding with either of the two hostile parties, yet when they know us better, they will hasten to us with all their hearts. But woe upon woe to those who will unite with the Mamlūks and assist them in the war against us, for they will not find the way of escape, and no trace of them shall remain.

First Article

All the villages, situated within three hours' distance from the places through which the French army passes, are required to send to the Commander-in-Chief some persons, deputed by them, to announce to the aforesaid, that they submit and that they have hoisted the French flag, which is white, blue, and red.

Second Article

Every village that shall rise against the French army, shall be burnt down.

Third Article

Every village that submits to the French army must hoist the French flag and also the flag of our friend the Ottoman Sultan, may he continue for ever.

Fourth Article

The Shaykh of each village must immediately seal all property, houses, and possessions, belonging to the Mamlūks, making the most strenuous effort that not the least thing be lost.

Fifth Article

The Shaykhs, Qāḍīs, and Imāms must remain / at their posts, and every countryman shall remain peaceably in his dwelling, and also prayers shall be performed in the mosques as customary and the Egyptians, all of them shall render thanks for God's graciousness, praise be to Him and may He be exalted, in extirpating the power of the Mamlūks, saying with a loud voice, May God perpetuate the glory of the Ottoman Sultan! May God preserve the glory of the French army! May God curse the Mamlūks and rightly adjust the condition of the Egyptian people.

Written in the Camp at Alexandria on the 13th of the month Messidor [the 6th year] of the founding of the French Republic, that is to say toward the end of the month Muḥarram in the year [1213] of the Hijra [2 July 1798].

It ends here word for word. Here is an explanation of the incoherent words and vulgar constructions which he put into this miserable letter.

His statement 'In the name of God, the Merciful, the Compassionate. There is no god but God. He has no son, nor has He an associate in

His Dominion'. In mentioning these three sentences there is an indication that the French agree with the three religions, but at the same time they do not agree with them, nor with any religion. They are consistent with the Muslims in stating the formula 'In the name of God', in denying that He has a son or an associate. They disagree with the Muslims in not mentioning the two Articles of Faith, in rejecting the mission of Muḥammad, and the legal words and deeds which are necessarily recognized by religion. They agree with the Christians in most of their words and deeds, but disagree with them by not mentioning the Trinity, and denying the mission and furthermore in rejecting their beliefs, killing the priests, and destroying the churches. Then, their statement 'On behalf of the French Republic, etc.', that is, this proclamation is sent from their Republic, that means their body politic, because they have no chief or sultan with whom they all agree, like others, whose function is to speak on their behalf. For when they rebelled against their sultan six years ago and killed him, the people agreed unanimously that there was not to be a single ruler but that their state, territories, laws, and administration of their affairs, should be in the hands of the intelligent and wise men among them. They appointed persons chosen by them and made them heads of the army, and below them generals and commanders of thousands, two hundreds, and tens, administrators and advisers, on condition that they were all to be equal and none superior to any other in view of the equality of creation and nature. They made this the foundation and basis of their system. This is the meaning of their statement 'based upon the foundation of liberty and equality'. Their term 'liberty' means that they are not slaves like the Mamlūks; 'equality' has the aforesaid meaning. Their officials are distinguished by the cleanliness of their garments. They wear emblems on their uniforms and upon their heads. For example an Amīr of ten has a large rosette[38] of silk upon his head / like a big rose. If he is a commander of twenty-five his rosette is of two colours, and if he is a commander of a hundred his rosette is of three colours. His hat which is known as *burnayṭa* (It. *borreta*) is embroidered with gold brocade, or he may bear upon his shoulders an emblem of the same. If he has a reputation for daring and is well-known for his heroism and has been wounded several times he receives two badges on his shoulder. They follow this rule: great and small, high and low, male and female are all equal. Sometimes they break this rule according to their whims and inclinations or reasoning. Their women do not veil themselves and have no modesty; they do not care whether they uncover their private parts. Whenever a Frenchman has to perform an act of nature he does so wherever he happens to be, even in full view of people, and he goes away as he is, without washing his private parts after defecation. If he is a man of taste and refinement[39] he wipes himself with whatever he finds, even with a paper with writing on it, otherwise he remains as he is. They have intercourse with any woman who pleases them and vice versa. Sometimes one of their women goes into a barber's shop, and invites him to shave her pubic hair.[40] If he wishes he can take his fee in kind. It is their custom to shave both their moustaches and beard. Some of them leave the hair of their cheeks only.

They do not shave their heads nor their pubic hair. They mix their foods. Some might even put together in one dish coffee, sugar, arrack,[41] raw eggs, limes, and so on. As for the name 'Bonaparté' this is the title of their general, it is not a name. Its meaning is 'the pleasant gathering', because *Bona* (*Būnā*) means 'pleasant' and *parté* means 'gathering'. His statement 'for a long time' is a redundant adverb *(ẓarf laghw)* connected with his saying 'have treated' and the implication underlying the statement is that the Ṣanjaqs who are ruling over Egypt have been treating for a long time, etc. *Ṣanājiq* is the plural of *Ṣanjāq*, he is so called with reference to the banner which is displayed over his head. Sometimes the *ṣād* is changed into *sīn*. The correct form of '*yatasalṭanū*' is *yatasalṭanūn* (to rule), because there is no reason to omit the *nūn*. The same applies to *yata'āmalū* (to treat). His statement 'basely and contemptuously' is connected with an elision which again is connected with his statement *fī ḥaqq*, and the implication is that 'they give treatment with baseness and contempt'. But if he were to say *yu'āmilūn al-Faransāwiyya bi 'l-dhull wa 'l-iḥtiqār* (they treat the French basely and contemptuously), it would be most excellently and succinctly expressed. In fact the French are more deserving of such a treatment. His statement *Faḥaḍara* (Therefore has come) there is no reason for this *fā* here. Good style would require *wa-qad ḥaḍara* (it has come). The word *al-ān* (now) is in the accusative, being an adverb modifying the verb *ḥaḍara* (has come) and *sā'a* (the hour) is a subject. So the meaning is: 'the hour of their punishment has now come'. It is much better to delete the word now (*al-ān*), the adverb being redundant, because *al-ān* is a noun denoting present time, and it is the same as the hour of punishment. It requires some constraint to turn it into a simple adverb of time, may God afflict them with every calamity. His statement *Wā ḥasratan* (Unfortunately), probably it is *wa-khuṣuṣan* (especially), because this word has no place here, / for *wā ḥasratan* is a word expressing affliction and the context does not permit it here. Its occurrence here is like animal droppings on the road or a boulder in a mountain pass, may God afflict the man who composed it with break-bone fever[42] and may God expose him to all sorts of destruction. His statement 'for ages' is connected with his statement 'have acted corruptly' (*yufsidū*) which is corrupt like all former and later verbs in the imperfect, because the *nūn* has been omitted. The expression should be read as *yufsidūn min muddat 'uṣūr* (they have been corrupting for ages). He qualifies the ages as long in order to clarify and explain. However, *'uṣūr* is the plural of *'aṣr* (age), *'aṣr* means time, and so if they are numerous ages they are long. The correct form of *al-majlūbīn* is *al-majlūbūn* (imported), because it is an adjective qualifying the *zumra* (group), or it is *na't maqṭū'* (an adjective cut off from its qualified noun).

His statement *alladhī yūwjad* (that is to be found) should be *alladhī lā yūwjad* (that is not to be found). The expression is not complete without *lā*.

His statement *fa-ammā Rabb al-'ālamīn* (However the Lord of the Universe) is recommencement: 'the Almighty', (indeed He is), and one aspect and clear sign of His great power is bringing these devils to the fertile land of the kings and sultans, and their discomfiture and their destruction.

His saying *qad ḥattama* etc. (has decreed) shows that they are appointing themselves controllers of God's secrets, but there is no disgrace worse than disbelief. *Yā ayyuhā 'l-Miṣriyyīn* should be *al-Miṣriyyūn*, because it is a vocative.

His statement '*qad yaqūlū lakum*' (they may say) refers to those who fabricate lies against us.

His saying *fī hādhā 'l-ṭaraf* (hither), means 'this part of the earth'. His statement *wa-qūlū li 'l-muftariyīn* (but tell the slanderers) is the plural of *muftarī* (slanderer) which means liar, and how worthy of this description they are. The proof of that is his saying 'I have not come to you except for the purpose of restoring your rights from the hands of the oppressors', which is the first lie he uttered and a falsehood which he invented. Then he proceeds to something even worse than that, may God cast him into perdition, with his words: 'I more than the Mamlūks serve God ...'. There is no doubt that this is a derangement of his mind, and an excess of foolishness. What a worship he is speaking about, however great its intensity, *kufr* (disbelief) had dulled his heart, and prevented him from reaching the way of his salvation. There is inversion in the words which should read *innanī a'budu Allāh akthar min al-Mamālīk* (I serve God more than the Mamlūks do). However, it is possible that there is no inversion, and that the meaning is 'I have more troops or more money than the Mamlūks' and that the accusative of specification has been omitted. So his words 'I serve God' are a new sentence and a new lie.

His statement '[I] revere His Prophet' is conjoined to what goes before, as one lie joined to another, because if he respected him he would believe in him, accept his truth, and respect his nation. His statement *al-Qur'ān al-'aẓīm* (the glorious Qur'ān) is joined to 'His Prophet', that is, 'I respect the glorious Qur'ān', and this too is a lie, because to respect the Qur'ān means to glorify it, and one glorifies it by believing / in what it contains. The Qur'ān is one of the miracles of the Prophet which proves his truth, and that he is the Prophet to the end of time, and that his nation is the most noble of all nations. These people deny all that and lie in every thing they enumerate, 'And many as are the signs in the Heavens and on the Earth, yet they will pass them by, and turn aside from them'.[43]

His saying '[all people] are equal in the eyes of God' the Almighty, this is a lie and stupidity. How can this be when God has made some superior to others as is testified by the dwellers in the Heavens and on the Earth?

In his statement *fa-huwa al-'aql* (it is the reason), there is no place for the *fā*, except that it is put in through the ignorance of the writer.

His statement *wa-bayn al-Mamālīk*, the word *bayn* is out of place and makes the language even more corrupt.

His saying *mā 'l-'aql* (what is there of reason), is a subject and predicate, and a rhetorical question. In this sentence there is an omission, that is 'to them', and the meaning is that the Mamlūks have no Reason.

His statement *kamā yaḥlū* (everything which sweetens) is an object to his word *yatamallakū* (to possess). His statement *Ḥaythumā* (wherever) is a new sentence, mentioned to enumerate the favours which the Mamlūks obtained.

His statement *fa 'l-yuwarrūnā* (let them then produce), this is a colloquial word which is not in accordance with Arabic style. His saying 'the title-deed, which God conferred upon them': this is base ignorance and *kufr* (heresy), because God does not give men possession of anything by writing a title-deed. What he means is that the people pass the country from hand to hand from their masters as these Mamlūks did, or from their masters' successors, or by conquest and compulsion. Prefixing *lākin* with *fa* is proof of ungrammatical language. The word *lākin* is as ungrammatical language as is the prefixing of *fa*.

As for his statement *'alā 'l-bashar* (toward mankind), it is more correct to say *bi 'l-bashar*, because the verb *ra'afa* (to show mercy) introduces its object with *bi*, but the verb *'adala* is intransitive.

His saying *bi-'awnih* (with the help of) is connected with his statement *lā yustathnā aḥad* (no one shall be excluded from) and so is his saying *min al-yawm* (from this day).

His statement *al-manāṣib al-sāmiya* (eminent positions), that means *al-murtafi'a* (elevated). This is in order to avert blame from themselves by giving high posts of authority to the low and vulgar people among them, as for example their appointment of Barṭulmān (Barthélemy) the artilleryman to the post of Katkhudā Mustaḥfiẓān. He says 'and thus the state of the whole population will be rightly adjusted'. Yes, that is to say, under the administration of wise and intelligent men. But they did not appoint them. The word *Muslimīn* should be *Muslimūn* in the nominative. The point of putting the word in the *naṣb* (accusative) has already been mentioned. There is another point namely: that their Islam is *naṣb* (fraud).

As for his statement 'and destroyed there the Papal See', by this deed they have gone against the Christians as has already been pointed out. So those people are opposed to both Christians and Muslims, and do not hold fast to any religion. You see that they are materialists, who deny all God's attributes, the Hereafter and Resurrection, and who reject Prophethood and Messengership. They believe that the world was not created, and that the heavenly bodies and the occurrences of the Universe are influenced by the movement of the stars, and that nations appear and states decline, according to the nature of the conjunctions and the aspects of the moon. Some believe in transmigration of souls, or other fantasies. For this reason they do not slaughter ritually any animal they eat / or behead any man, before having killed them, so that the parts of his soul may not be separated and scattered, so as not to be whole in another body, and similar nonsense and erroneous beliefs. The word *sanjāq* should be *ṣanjaq* without the *ā*.

His statement *btā' al-Mamālīk* (belonging to the Mamlūks) is despicable and a banal and trite word. The word *muṭma'in* should be *muṭma'inan* because it is *ḥāl* (circumstantial expression), and converting it to the nominative (*raf'*) incorrectly is an indication of their state, and their insignificance. May God hurry misfortune and punishment upon them, may He strike their tongues with dumbness, may He scatter their hosts, and disperse them, confound their intelligence, and cause their breath to cease. He has the power to do that, and it is up to Him to answer.

On Thursday the twenty-eighth, news arrived that the French had advanced towards Fuwwa and then al-Raḥmāniyya.

On Sunday the first of Ṣafar, news came that on Friday the twenty-ninth the Egyptian army had encountered that of the French but after a short while Murād Bey and his army were routed for they were not able to hold their ground. However only a small number of men from both armies were killed. The *dhayabiyya* of Murād Bey went up in flames, arsenal, equipment, and all. The commander of the artillery was also burnt to death. When Murād Bey saw what had happened, he ran away, leaving all his belongings and a number of cannons. His soldiers immediately followed suit and indeed there was a great number with him. Once news of these events spread, great alarm took hold of the people and Ibrāhīm Bey set out on horseback for Būlāq, where the Shaykhs and men of distinction gathered around him. There they discussed this event, and arrived at a joint decision to erect fortifications extending from Būlāq to Shubrā. Ibrāhīm Bey and the Pasha were to take position behind these barricades together with their Ṣanjaqs: Ibrāhīm Bey the younger, Sulaymān Bey, Ayyūb Bey the elder, Qāsim Bey, Qāsim Bey the second, Marzūq Bey, 'Uthmān Bey al-Ashqar, and others bringing with them their Kāshifs and Amīrs.

On Monday, Murād Bey disembarked at the Jīza, where he began setting up entrenchments on the west bank, extending from Bashtīl to the end of Inbāba. He undertook this task with his Ṣanjaqs, Amīrs, and a group of his Khushdāshs, attending personally to the management and organization of affairs together with 'Alī Pasha al-Ṭarābulsī. He began to pay the soldiers out of his own pocket. Naṣūḥ Pasha was also with him. All the while they moved their household effects from their large houses to smaller ones, and on to ships bearing southward. They sent for camels to bear their loads. On Tuesday, a general call to arms was proclaimed, and the people were summoned to the entrenchments. This call was repeated / time and time again. People closed their shops and markets, and everyone was in an uproar. The noise and confusion were very great. Some of the people said that this was by Imperial

The battle of the Pyramids: Mourad Bey leading the Dugua division
(Detail of a picture by Vivant Denon)

order and that the French were accompanied by Pashas sent by the Sultan. Most of the rural population and fallaḥīn believed this because of the proclamation mentioned above which the French distributed throughout the country. The Shaykhs, the dignitaries, and the common people set out with clubs and arms. The price of arms, gunpowder, and bullets increased greatly.

The price of a *raṭl* of gunpowder rose to sixty *paras* (*niṣf fiḍḍa*,) and that of bullets ninety *dirhams*; the same applied even to clubs.

People set up at Būlāq, some in houses, some in mosques, and some in tents. As for the common people, and those who couldn't find a place to stay, they would retire to their own houses at night, returning to the camp in the morning. Ibrāhīm Bey sent for the bedouin such as the tribes of Bilī, al-Ḥuwayṭāt, al-Ṣawāliḥa, al-Ḥabāyba and others. He commanded them to take the front positions. In addition the bedouin of al-Hannādī, some of the bedouin of Upper Egypt, al-Khabīrī, Ṭarhūna, and others, came to Murād Bey's camp. Thus every day the throng increased and the terror with them. The city was vacated, the dust accumulated in the market-places, because there was no one to sweep them or to splash water, and the shops were abandoned. Gangs of thugs looting, as well as other hooligans, thieves, pickpockets, robbers, highwaymen, all having a field day. Relations between people ceased, and all dealings and business came to a standstill. The roads in the city became insecure, not to mention those outside it. Violence flared up in the countryside, and people began to kill each other. They stole cattle and plundered fields. They set fire to the barns and sought to avenge old hatreds and blood feuds, and so on.

Moreover, in the same month, they sought out the Europeans who were living in Egypt, such as the French and Austrians, and then imprisoned some of them in the Citadel, and others in the houses of the Amīrs. They began to search for arms in places belonging to the Europeans. They repeated the proclamation that everyone was to go to the entrenchments while every day the news and rumours increased about the advancing French. And on Friday the sixth of the month, the French reached al-Jisr al-Aswad. The people gathered on the banks, but most of the crowd formed on that of Būlāq. Meanwhile, the religious orders of mendicants (*faqīrs*) and the dervish banner-bearers also set out with their banners, flags, and clamour.

When Saturday morning dawned, and the French reached Umm Dīnār, the crowds thickened and the alarm increased, and an innumerable throng surpassing all description gathered at Būlāq and on its outskirts and in the southern and northern districts. A crowd also formed on the bank of Inbāba, but smaller in number. The Ghuzz, the soldiers, and the Mamlūks gathered on the two banks, but they were irresolute, and were at odds with one another, being divided in opinion, envious of each other, frightened / for their lives, their well-being, and their comforts; immersed in their ignorance and self-delusion; arrogant and haughty in their attire and presumptuousness; afraid of decreasing in number, and pompous in their finery, heedless of the results of their action; contemptuous of their enemy, unbalanced in their reasoning and judgement. They were unlike the other group, that is the French, who were a complete contrast in everything mentioned above. They acted as if they were following the tradition of the Community (of Muḥammad) in early Islam and saw themselves as fighters in a holy war. They never considered the number of their enemy too high, nor did they care who among them was killed. Indeed they considered anyone who fled a traitor to his community, and an apostate to his faith and creed. They follow the orders of their commander and faithfully obey their leader. Their only shade is the hat on their head and their only mount their own two feet. Their food and drink is but a morsel and a sip, hanging under their arms. Their baggage and change of clothing hang on their backs like a pillow and when they sleep they lie on it as is usual. They have signs and signals among themselves which they all obey to the letter.

The assumption was that they would approach from both banks of the river, but during the midday rest of the above-mentioned Saturday a band of Egyptian soldiers rode in the direction of Bashtīl and met the French, charging upon them, so the French fired at them in successive volleys. Then the Egyptians retreated to the area of the entrenchments. The cannons were fired from both sides. So a group of Amīrs on horseback began to cross to the western bank. They jostled each other on the ferry-boats. There was only one crossing-place, but it was filled with beams of timber. Also some *qawāwīs* and *ḥarārīq* boats were there, ready for pleasure trips, but because of their bad planning and mismanagement, they had not prepared themselves for crossing. Moreover, a side wind increased in force, and the waves reached a peak of turmoil. The sand rose in clouds, which the wind blew into the faces of the Egyptian soldiers. Some crossed and waited for the horses, but others were kept back by the wind, and their boats got stuck in the sand-bank which was in the middle of the river, hidden by the height of the water. As for the French, a troop of them approached the Egyptian entrenchment from the front. The Egyptians mounted their horses and fought them. While they were engaged with this troop of French soldiers they did not notice that suddenly another group infiltrated the western channel and appeared behind the entrenchments, firing cannons.

The Egyptians went back and fought with them for about three-quarters of an hour and the rifles of the French were like a boiling pot on a fierce fire. Then the Egyptians were defeated and fled back to al-Jīza. Murād Bey went up to his place and attended to his affairs for about a quarter of an hour; then he rode southwards, his soldiers and his Mamlūks following him. Meanwhile, the bank of Būlāq had become a seething mass of people of every description, high and low. They formed into groups, chewing their fingers out of distress and sorrow because they could not cross in the absence of ferry-boats. All that they were able to do was to raise cries of 'O God, O God', and 'Our sufficiency is God, and He is an excellent protector',[44] and the like. Their clamour and tumult / reached such a peak that it seemed as if they were fighting a battle of noise and yells.

When Ibrāhīm Bey, the Pasha, and those who were with them at the entrenchments saw that the people on the western bank were defeated not only did they not stand firm in their positions, but they took to flight on horseback abandoning the entrenchments, tents, cannons, and all, setting out in the direction of al-'Ādiliyya. Then the French, once they had captured the western entrenchments and the galleons of Murād Bey, immediately directed the mouths of the cannons towards the eastern bank and furthermore shot at the Egyptians with bullets. When the people saw that Ibrāhīm Bey and his followers had fled and that the continuous barrages of fire were directed towards them, they themselves fled to Būlāq and towards Cairo. In their great alarm they took to their heels and ran like the waves of the sea in such a way that the cleverest among them became he who ran faster than his neighbour. Most of the notables abandoned their [field] kitchens, tents, and furnishings. The dust which covered the area thickened around them because of the force of their tramping, their great number, and the strength of the wind, blinding them and throwing them into confusion. Their cries and lamentings rose up from far and near. They entered the city crowd after crowd and the women, singly and in pairs, wailed from the windows. People bumped into one another, the yelling, clamour, and rage becoming tremendous. Most of them made up their minds to vacate the city and leave Cairo. Some of them exclaimed: 'Let us go to al-Shām', others cried out: 'Let us go to Upper Egypt or the Suez!'. When Ibrāhīm Bey reached al-'Ādiliyya he sent for his womenfolk and those of the Amīrs and others who were with him. Most of the Mamlūks left on foot, leading their women on horses. Some of them rode bareback. Two or three young Mamlūks could be seen riding on one horse. When the sun set that day the French were in al-Jīza. Glory be to God, the Doer, the Almighty.

Nobody died in that battle except Ayyūb Bey al-Daftardār and Ibrāhīm Bey al-Wālī, who threw himself with his horse into the river and was drowned. In addition three Kāshifs and about twenty Mamlūks perished, and a number of them were taken prisoner. Some of the galleon soldiers (*'askar ghaylūnjiyya*), and common people died as well. So the Egyptian army altogether disappointed whatever hopes had been placed in it and brought upon themselves both the fires of Hell and disgrace; 'judgement is with God, the One, the Almighty'.[45]

Night fell and the inhabitants of the city were in a great confusion and a fantastic uproar, moving things from place to place, carrying and transporting. In the evening, a rumour spread among the people that the French had crossed to Būlāq and had put it to the torch, as well as al-Jīza. The fear and terror of the populace waxed greater than ever, the reason being that some of the sailors had set fire to one of the three galleons belonging to Murād Bey, on the bank of Inbāba. When Murād Bey left al-Jīza he ordered that the big galleon be towed southward but south of al-Jīza the Nile was muddy for the water was shallow there. There was a great number of war-machines and much ammunition in this galleon, and for this reason he ordered it to be set on fire. The flames swelled up towards the clouds, and when the people of the city beheld the blaze of the fire from the direction of al-Jīza and Būlāq, they thought, or rather, were certain that the French had set fire to both places. So the people were in great confusion and perplexity in addition to the fear, panic, and alarm which possessed them. Some made up their minds to move and took counsel to this effect. Some were determined to leave, while others decided to stay where they were. Still others concealed their decision from their friends and neighbours, trying to escape from their relatives and companions, fearing lest they say: 'Take me' or 'Carry me with you'. Thus they deceived their fellows and travelled with those who were leaving. / When the first watch of the night had elapsed one of Shaykh 'Abd Allāh al-Sharqāwī's[46] friends advised him to depart, because the French had reached Bāb al-Ḥadīd, crossed it, and set it on fire, and were at that moment looting there, killing the residents of that quarter, and raping their women. He went on to say 'If we hesitate, they will reach us within two hours'. So Shaykh 'Abd Allāh sent someone to Shaykh al-Sādāt to alarm him, and arouse his anxiety, and urge him to ride away quickly. So he carried [with him] those possessions which were portable and necessary, and set out with him on horseback from Bāb al-Barqiyya. Others who rode out that night were Shaykh 'Umar al-Naqīb, Shaykh al-Amīr,[47] Shaykh al-Bakrī,[48] the Ruzmānjī[49] (Controller), a number of effendis, grandees, notables and merchants and the like, taking their womenfolk with them. When the news spread among the common people about their riding off they became even more anxious and frightened than before and they determined to escape and follow them in their flight. But the fact remained that the notables did not know which road to take, in which direction to go, or in which place to settle. Meanwhile the common people vied with one another in leaving their homes, residences, and living quarters, appearing from all directions and calling out to each other. One would exclaim 'Come down, O Ḥajj Muḥammad', or 'Come along, Abū 'Alī!'. In a like manner the women shouted to their friends and acquaintances, addressing them by name and *kunya*. One of them would say: 'Come down, Umm Ḥasan!', 'Come along Umm 'Aisha! Bring your daughter and come on!', and things of this kind, as if they thought that the people were going on an outing to al-Rawḍa and the Nilometer. A large number of people left in this way; those who found no mount on which to ride or on which to load their household possessions, left on foot, carrying their baggage on their heads. Those who had the means and could find a donkey or some other beast, bought it at several times its value. Some went on foot themselves while their wives or daughters rode! Most of the women left unveiled, carrying their children in the darkness of night, and continued in this fashion all through Sunday night and the next morning. They took with them all the money, baggage, and household furnishings they could carry, but once they had left the gates of Cairo behind, and were in the open countryside the bedouin and fallaḥīn confronted them, plundering most of them, robbing them of their possessions, their camels, and their money, in such great quantities as to be innumerable and incalculable: so much that without a doubt the property which left Cairo on that night was greater than that which remained in it. This was because most of the property was in the possession of the Amīrs, grandees, and notables, together with their womenfolk; and in the heat of their excitement they had taken it all.

Most of those who were of modest means and those who were well off also left with whatever they had, while others who were hindered by disability or were too lazy to depart and who had any money or jewellery which was dear to them gave it to a neighbour or friend among those escaping. And the same applied to deposits and trusts belonging to the North African pilgrims and travellers, all of which were lost. Sometimes they killed anyone they could, or whoever did not easily surrender his clothing and possessions. They stripped the women of their clothing and violated them, including ladies and noblewomen. Some of the people returned home very soon after, and those were the ones who had delayed and heard what befell the first group. Others took a chance and went on, relying on their great numbers, supporters and guards, either surviving or perishing. During that night, things happened the like of which had never occurred in Cairo, neither did we ever hear of anything which resembled any of them in the earlier histories. As for Shaykh al-Sādāt[50] and Shaykh al-Sharqāwī, / when they saw this state of affairs and when the bedouin took two camels with their loads from the latter, they turned to al-Maṭariyya and sent for Abū Ṭawīla who arrived and warded off the bedouin who were surrounding them from all sides, and then continued to protect the two Shaykhs. Meanwhile Sayyid ʻUmar al-Naqīb, Shaykh al-Amīr, and Shaykh Sālim Masʻūd, the chief of the Maghrib residence (at al-Azhar), all went to the camp of Ibrāhīm Bey, after (the bedouin) had taken the possessions of Shaykh Sālim and those of his womenfolk as well as deposits which they had with them, all of which were lost. Sunday morning found the people surging like waves against each other, expecting disaster to strike, but it became clear that the French had not crossed over to the eastern bank, and that the fire came from the ships which were mentioned before. At this point a group of scholars and others assembled at al-Azhar and deliberated amongst themselves. They agreed to send a letter to the French and await the reply. So they sent for one of the notables of Tripoli, a man called ʻAlī Bey, who was resident in Cairo and knew the French language and with him they sent another man from the Maghrib residence in al-Azhar and yet another from among the *ʻulamā'* (*min al-mutaʻammimīn*).[51] They went to Būlāq with the intention of boarding a boat to the western bank. But it happened that the French fired some cannons by accident, so they did not dare to cross, and went back. But that Maghribī, known as Abū 'l-Qāsim, took the letter and crossed to the opposite bank where he met with their chief and gave him the letter. The chief then asked through the translator 'Why didn't one of your Shaykhs come to us?'. He answered 'I came here to get permission for them to come and obtain safe-conduct both for them and for the people'. The chief replied: 'We have already sent you a letter which should suffice, and we won't write another one'. So the above-mentioned Abū 'l-Qāsim went back and informed the Shaykhs, saying 'A group of your notables must surely go'. So the Shaykhs Muṣṭafā al-Ṣāwī, Sulaymān al-Fayyūmī,[52] and others went and crossed to the bank of Inbāba. But they found that the French had gone to the palace of Murād Bey in al-Jīza. So they went after them and met their chief who received them very honourably and smiled at them, giving assurances of safe-conduct. They said 'We want you to write an assurance of safe-conduct for the people'. He replied 'We have already sent it to you'. They reiterated 'It is essential that we get it so that the people and the subject be set at ease'. So they wrote another paper for them, saying 'From the camp of al-Jīza, addressed to the people of Cairo. We have already sent you a letter which should suffice. We stated that we came here only for the purpose of exterminating the Mamlūks who treated the French in a humiliating manner and contemptuously, and who robbed the merchants and the Sultan of their property. When we reached the western bank, they came out against us, so we received them as befitted them. We killed some of them and imprisoned others, who are now with us. Some of them escaped and we are searching for them and will continue until not a single one of them remains in Egypt. But the Shaykhs, the *'ulamā'*, the people of rank, and the subjects will be left in peace', and thus the letter went on until the end with their twisted words and pompous expressions. Then he told them: 'I want seven of you to become advisers and administrators, who will appear every day before the man in charge of the Dīwān; and another two to act as couriers and to carry out various tasks. You must also appoint people to be in charge of the various functions of government and administration'. They told him 'Our leading Shaykhs panicked and left Cairo'. He asked 'What for? Write to them and call them back'. So they wrote several letters of safe-conduct, on his authority ordering them to present themselves, and that meeting continued until sunset. Meanwhile, the people were saying 'We wonder what has happened to them'. When the Shaykhs returned in the evening with those messages and in front of them a herald declaring safe-conduct, the people felt somewhat reassured. Next morning they sent those letters of safe-conduct to the Shaykhs with the result that Shaykh al-Sādāt and al-Sharqāwī arrived / from al-Maṭariyya, as well as al-Bakrī who came from where he had been last Thursday. But al-Naqīb did not trust the letter, and went with Ibrāhīm Bey. The same happened with Shaykh Sālim and the Ruznāmjī and those who were with them, such as 'Uthmān Efendī al-'Abbāsī, Muḥammad Efendī the second *qalfa*,[53] and others. Shaykh al-Amīr did not arrive either.

On that day the loafers and the rabble gathered into a mob and plundered the house of Ibrāhīm Bey, as well as that of Murād Bey in Qaysūn which they burned down. They also plundered several houses of the Amīrs and stole their contents, such as bedding, copper vessels, furniture, and other things, selling them at the cheapest prices.

On Thursday 13 Ṣafar they convened with the chief of the Dīwān and appointed for the presidency of the Dīwān ten persons, namely Shaykh al-Sharqāwī, Shaykh al-Bakrī, Shaykh Muṣṭafā al-Ṣawī, Shaykh Sulaymān al-Fayyūmī, Shaykh Mūsā al-Sirsī,[54] Shaykh Muḥammad al-Mahdī,[55] Shaykh Muṣṭafā al-Damanhūrī,[56] Shaykh Aḥmad al-'Arīshī,[57] Shaykh Yūsuf al-Shubrakhītī, Shaykh Muḥammad al-Dawākhilī. However, Shaykh al-Sādāt did not come with them because of a slight indisposition resulting from this affair and related events. The Katkhudā (deputy, lieutenant) al-Bāshā and the Qāḍī al-'Askar also came. They made Muḥammad Aghā al-Muslimānī Katkhudā Mustaḥfiẓān, 'Alī Aghā al-Sha'rāwī the Wālī, and Ḥasan Aghā Muḥarram the Muḥtasib (market superintendent), this after a long argument in which the French said that no one of Mamlūk stock could hold a position. The Shaykhs replied that the people of Cairo feared only the Mamlūk race and that the above-mentioned were of the veteran Shūrbajīs[58] and the old (Mamlūk) houses.[59] They appointed as Katkhudā[60] to the Ṣārī 'Askar Zayn al-Fiqār the Katkhudā of Muḥammad Bey al-Alfī. Among the French counsellors Caffe and Geloi[61] and the deputy of the *dawāwīn al-mukūs* (customs duty bureaux) was Ḥanna Benoît.[62] On that day, General Bonaparte crossed to the Cairo side and settled in al-Azbakiyya in the house of Muḥammad Bey al-Alfī, who had built and constructed it in al-Sākit district that same year. Moreover he had furnished it splendidly and has laid down fine carpets. The women left, abandoning all that it contained. The French entered it, stepping on the carpets with their shoes and sandals as was their custom, since they never take off their

Bonaparte entering Cairo (Engraving by Raffet)

shoes with which they tread upon filth, not even when they sleep! Among their repulsive habits also is their practice of spitting and blowing their noses upon the furnishings. Their etiquette, however, is such that whenever one of them blows his nose or spits he rubs it with his shoes and so on.

During that day the members of the Dīwān went to the house of the chief of the Dīwān, wherein he told them about the plundering of houses which had taken place. They replied 'Those who acted thus are mere rabble and riff-raff'. The French asked 'Why are they doing this after we ordered you to guard the houses, to seal off the property of the Mamlūks, and to stop those who oppose this effectively?'. They replied 'This is a matter which we had not the power to prevent, for indeed it is the business of the rulers'. So the Wālī and the Aghā went and declared safe-conduct, and asked the people to open the shops and to stop the plundering. But they did not stop and the shops continued to be closed, the markets empty, and the roads dusty. The French started to open the houses of the Amīrs, to enter and loot them to their hearts' content, then depart, leaving the doors open. After them the rabble entered and cleaned out what remained. This went on for several days. Then they sought out the houses of the Amīrs and their *mamlūks* (*atbā'*)[63] sealing off some of them and occupying others. The members of the corps of Ujāqs and inhabitants who feared for their houses hung a flag on their doors and got a handwritten paper (from the French) which they posted on their doors, without knowing what was written on it.

In that month they invested Barthélemy, the European soldier, as Katkhudā Mustaḥfiẓān. He was one of the lowliest of the European soldiers living in Cairo. He served with the artillerymen of Muḥammad Bey al-Alfī. He had a shop in al-Mūskī where he sold long-necked glass bottles in his spare time. He was known as *Farṭ al-Rummān* (Pomegranate Seeds). When he was invested with this post at the house of the Ṣārī 'Askar, he went out in a procession / riding a horse with its saddle decked with a decorated cover (*qallā'iyya*).[64] In front of him marched a great number of soldiers whom they had assigned to him; among these were the Ghuzz, unemployed soldiers, and the Ilḍashāt,[65] all of them Muslims. Upon his head he wore a rose of silk, and servants with silver lances surrounded him. He had a Biyuk Bāshī and guards and every senior had several soldiers under him. Then they allocated places to them in which they were to live. All of them were under his supreme authority. He took the house of Yaḥyā Kāshif al-Kabīr which belonged to Ibrāhīm Bey and occupied it with all the furniture, household effects, and slave girls in it. They appointed another Frenchman and made him Amīn al-Baḥrayn (the holder of the two ports of Old Cairo and Būlāq), and another whom they appointed *Aghāt al-Risāla* (delivery Aghā), and others to Sawāḥil al-Ghilla (the river banks of the granaries), and the special Dīwān. The chief of the Dīwān occupied the house of Qāyit Aghā in al-Azbakiyya, where the Dīwān meets, and the Shaykhs and others attend. The Governor (Qā'im Maqām) of Cairo known as Dupuy settled in the house of Ibrāhīm Bey al-Wālī, Shaykh al-Balad,[66] in the house of Ibrāhīm Bey al-Kabīr, Magallon in that of Murād Bey at the quay of al-Khashshāb and the Ruznāmjī in the old house of Shaykh al-Bakrī. The Copts used to assemble at his place. They asked for the registers of the Ruznāma and kept them. The Daftardār and others also (used to assemble there). All of them were Europeans. Moreover their soldiers entered the city gradually, until the streets were full of them. They lived in the houses and the quarters stank of them, but they did not disturb anybody, and they used to buy goods at artificially high prices. They sold one egg for one *para*, while before they had been four at one *para*. The people opened several shops next to them for all kinds of foodstuffs such as pastry, cakes, fried fish, and the like. The Greek Christian grocers opened several shops for selling alcoholic beverages such as wine and arrack, and several taverns and coffee-houses, and pedlars (also came). This became very excessive.

In that (month) the Shaykhs pleaded for the prisoners of the Mamlūks. They accepted their plea and released them. The prisoners, who numbered about twelve, entered the Mosque of al-Azhar in the worst condition, wearing torn blue clothes. They remained there living on the charitable gifts of the students of al-Azhar and begging from the passers-by. In that there is a moral for those who pay heed.

On Saturday they held the Dīwān. The outcome was a request for a loan amounting to five hundred thousand *riyāls*: two hundred thousand from the coffee merchants, one hundred thousand from the Shāmī Christians, the same from the European merchants, and the same from the Copt secretaries. They asked for a reduction but it was impossible; so they began to collect the amount.

And on that day, they called upon anyone who had taken goods from the looted houses ordering him to bring the stolen property to the residence of the Qā'im Maqām lest most unfortunate consequences befall him. In addition they proclaimed a safe-conduct for the wives of the Amīrs, telling them to return to live in their own houses and declare what they held of their husbands' property. In case they did not hold any of their husbands' property, they should come to settle the terms of their return so that they then might reside safely in their homes. Consequently, Nafīsa, the wife of Murād Bey appeared out of hiding and came to a settlement (*ṣālaḥat*) on behalf of herself and her followers among the wives of the Amīrs and Kāshifs, at a sum of one hundred and twenty thousand [*riyāl*] *farānsa* of which two hundred thousand *riyāls* were on her own behalf.

She began to raise the required funds from other women as well as from her own means. The French directed their request for money to her and in the same way to the rest of the women through intermediaries, and in this manner they collected a great deal. As a result the function of the Dīwān became simply the prevention of criminal acts, financial settlements, and the writing of letters of safe-conduct for the Ghuzz who were hiding in the villages so that they would present themselves and come to a settlement. Many of those who acted as intermediaries profited from this situation, as for example the Shāmi Christians, resident Europeans, and the like, who soon started making promises and dire threats, playing tricks, and so on, actions which are too diverse to be described at length.

On Sunday they demanded horses, camels, and weapons and thus collected a good number of these, even cows / and oxen, and as in the case of the settlements they collected a great deal.

They extended the search for the stock requested to the extent of breaking into many shops in the market of the armourers and the like, appropriating weapons without paying. Every day they would carry off household goods, upholstery, chests, saddles, and other things which are too many to be accounted for, on camels and donkeys. They would also discover and take away things which were hidden. They further engaged the services of builders, architects, and servants who knew the houses of their lords, so that they might reveal the places of hidden goods and treasures. On the same day they arrested Shaykh al-Ju'aydiyya (the chief of the ruffians) and another one with him, having them both shot in the Birkat al-Azbakiyya, as well as other persons at al-Rumayla. They brought back much loot.

On Tuesday they summoned the guilds of merchantmen in the bazaars and imposed upon them a large sum which they were unable to pay claiming that this was to be a loan to be repaid after sixty days. So they raised hue and cry and asked for help, going to the Mosque of al-Azhar and the shrine of al-Ḥusaynī where they called upon the Shaykhs who spoke with (the French) interceding on their behalf. As a result the loan was reduced to half, and they also extended the time of payment.

On the same day they ordered that the by-streets and gates leading to the alleys be opened, and scattered groups of their soldiers set out to pull down and break to pieces the gates of the by-streets and lanes. And so they continued for many a day in this activity in spite of the peoples' anxiety and the rumours that the French soldiers were intent upon killing the people during the Friday prayer or other fantasies of this kind.

That happened after they had achieved a certain degree of security and some shops had already opened. With the occurrence of these two episodes they withdrew into themselves once more.

On the twentieth of the same month the letters of the pilgrims arrived from al-'Aqaba, so the members of the Dīwān went to the Bāsh 'Askar (chief of staff) and informed him about this matter asking for safe-conduct for the Amīr al-Ḥājj. He refused, saying 'I will only grant him safe-conduct on condition that he comes without Mamlūks, as an ordinary person'. They asked him 'Who then will escort the pilgrims?'. He replied 'We will send them four thousand soldiers who will escort them to Egypt'. And so they wrote courteous letters requesting the Amīr al-Ḥājj to escort the pilgrims to Dār al-Ḥamra and as for afterwards all would be well. The letters had hardly reached the pilgrims before those of Ibrāhīm Bey arrived bearing exaggerated warnings and calling upon them to come to Bilbays.

So they directed themselves to Bilbays and spent some days there. Meanwhile Ibrāhīm Bey and those who were with him departed for Ṣuwwa and sent the women to al-Qurayn.

On the twenty-third of that month a group of French soldiers set out in the direction of al-'Ādiliyya and every day another group set out for the East. On Wednesday evening of the twenty-sixth the Bāsh 'Askar set out while the first groups reached al-Khānkah and Abū Za'bal. These groups, having arrived demanded impost for the upkeep of the military from Abū Za'bal. The inhabitants refused so (the soldiers) attacked and defeated them and looted the city, setting it on fire, then passing on to Bilbays. As for the pilgrims, during their stay in Bilbays, some of the fallaḥīn among them hired bedouin to deliver them to their districts of residence such as al-Gharbiyya and al-Manūfiyya. Others, who were not fallaḥīn, engaged the services of bedouin to bring them to Sharqiyyat al-Manṣūra / and al-Manūfiyya. Thus they dispersed throughout the land with their women, others staying at Bilbays. Ṣāliḥ Bey joined Ibrāhīm Bey with a group of merchants and other companions.

On the twenty-eighth the French took Bilbays where there was still a number of pilgrims left. They did not disturb them, but sent them to Cairo accompanied by a group of their soldiers.

Late Sunday night the messenger reached the Amīrs who were at Ṣuwwa, informing them that the French were coming upon them. So they rode out at midnight and went up in the direction of al-Qurayn, and abandoned the merchants and owners of goods. At daybreak a number of bedouin Shaykhs came to (the merchants) and made an agreement with them that they would deliver them to al-Qurayn, giving an oath to them that they would not betray them. Once they reached half-way they broke their oath and betrayed them, plundered their loads, dividing the goods among themselves, and stripped them of their clothes. Among these merchants was Sayyid Aḥmad al-Maḥrūqī, the merchants' Shāh Bandar, whose property was worth about three hundred thousand *riyāl farānsa* in cash and goods. The bedouin greatly mistreated them most evilly. When the French soldiers overtook them Sayyid Aḥmad al-Maḥrūqī went accompanied by a group of hypocritical bedouin and met the Ṣārī 'Askar and complained to him of what had befallen him and his companions. The Ṣārī 'Askar in turn rebuked them for their travelling and relying upon the Mamlūks and the bedouin. Then he arrested Abū Khashaba, the Shaykh of al-Qurayn, and commanded him 'Inform me of the whereabouts of the stolen goods'. The Shaykh replied 'Send a group to al-Qurayn with me'. When he arrived at al-Qurayn with the group he led them to some loads which the French took and divided among themselves. Then they followed him to another place where he had them believe that he would enter a certain spot from which he would bring them more loads, but he escaped from them without returning, and those soldiers returned with one load and a half, saying 'This is what we found and the man escaped from us'. The Ṣārī 'Askar replied 'We must get hold of this property'. They (the merchants) then asked for permission to return to Cairo and he sent with them a number of soldiers to accompany them and deliver them (safely) to Cairo and the merchants were at this point in the worst state possible. In addition there was with them a group of women who had set out on the night of the incident and they were in a heartrending condition as French soldiers dragged them to the city.

The month of Rabī' al-Awwal

On the second of this month the French arrived at the outskirts of eastern Qurayn while Ibrāhīm Bey and those accompanying him had already reached al-Sāliḥiyya (where they) left their loads and women, and placed the responsibility for their safety with the bedouin. However, some of the bedouin informed the French where the loads were placed, so the Ṣārī 'Askar set out taking with him the cavalry, intending to take the loads out of his over-confidence. Ibrāhīm and the Ghuzz learned of this, so he and Ṣāliḥ Bey plus a number of Amīrs and *mamlūks* set out riding and encountered (the French) with whom they battled with swords for a short time, after which the French were on the verge of defeat. Suddenly the news reached Ibrāhīm Bey that the bedouin had made for the loads (at once) and started to plunder them. So he and those who were with him returned to where he came from and caught up with the bedouin and attacked them chasing them away from his property and killing many of them. After this he journeyed to Qaṭiyya while the leader of the French army returned to Cairo, leaving a number of his troops dispersed throughout the country. He arrived at Cairo during the night, that being the night of Thursday, the fourth of the month.

On Friday the fifth, / coinciding with the thirteenth of Misrā (the twelfth month of the) Coptic calendar, the blessed Nile reached its full flood and the French leader gave orders to make the usual preparations and decorate (the boat called) *al-'Aqaba* and a number of ships and galleons. They called upon the people to go outside and to stroll along the Nile and to the Nilometer as was customary demanding this in spite of what had suddenly come upon them, as for example poll-taxes, unrelenting demands, looting of homes, harassing women, and girls, arresting and imprisoning them, and making financial settlements (*muṣālaḥāt*) which exceeded all bounds. The (French) Ṣārī 'Askar sent instructions to the Katkhudā 'l-Bāshā and the Qāḍī and to the Shaykhs who were members of the Council and high officials and so forth, to present themselves the next morning. He rode forth with them accompanied by his procession, decorations, troops, drums and pipes, to the palace of Qanṭarat al-Sadd, and the dam was cut in their presence. Then they celebrated with fireworks and shooting of cannons until the waters flowed into the canal (of Cairo), then the Ṣārī 'Askar rode with those accompanying him and returned to his house. And not a single person went out that night for pleasure excursions in boats as was customary except for Shāmī Christians, Copts, Europeans with their wives, and a few idlers[67] who went as onlookers in the morning, broken-hearted and despondent.

On that day the news repeated itself, in that a number of English ships reached the port of Alexandria and fought a naval battle with the French soldiers. Several days had passed since the news spread and it had already been discussed by the people, which embarrassed the French. And it happened that some Shāmī Christian merchants quoted someone by the name of Sayyid Aḥmad al-Zarw a merchant belonging to the Khān of Soap Merchants situated at al-Jamāliyya, as having discussed this affair. So the French ordered that he be brought before them and reminded him of what he had said but he denied it saying 'I heard it from So-and-so, the Christian', with the result that they also brought him before them and ordered that both of them have their tongues cut out, or that each one pay one hundred *riyāl faransa*. The Shaykhs interceded on their behalf but the French would not accept. So some of the Shaykhs asked, 'Set them free and we will bring you the money'. He said 'Non, non', and so Shaykh Muṣṭafā al-Ṣāwī sent for and received two hundred *riyāls faransa* and paid them on the spot. After the head of the Dīwān had counted out the money he returned it to the Shaykhs, saying 'Distribute the money among your poor'. So the original possessor of the money got it back and pretended that he had distributed it as (the head of the Dīwān) had ordered. So the people ceased to talk about this affair (of the French defeat).

The story of these English is that they are enemies of the French people, and that the French, when they attacked the Banādiqa, the Wandīk, and al-Jūrna (the Venetians, Venice, and Leghorn) and other places, also intended to attack the English but they could not reach them by land. So they fought them on the sea but were unable to withstand them, for the English are known for their strength and valour in sea battles, while the French are just the opposite. So the French knew that they could not achieve their ends against the English except on land, and there was no way for them to achieve this except through India, and (of course) there is passage to India only through the Red Sea, and the English are aware of this, and when they found that the French had taken possession of Alexandria and had crossed Egyptian territory, they were certain that the French would get to them afterwards from that direction and then they would undoubtedly be in constant need of supplies and soldiers (to India). So the English followed them immediately with many ships bearing troops to Alexandria and attacked the ships which they found outside the port and Abū Qīr. They defeated them and burnt a great ship of theirs called *Niṣf al-Dunyā* (*la Moitié du Monde*)[68] which was armour-plated in brass and which bore their munitions and the riches which they removed from Rome and Malta. They also burnt a great powder-magazine, then remained in their ships in front of Alexandria, coming and going freely / eastwards and westward, lying in wait for the supplies coming to the French or those which they sent to their country and intercepting them.

On that day the French despatched many troops to the port of Alexandria and also to al-Sharqiyya and when the water flowed in the canal, (the French General) ordered that the dam of al-Azbakiyya be shut and in this way prevented the water from entering the pool, this because their camp, troops, and cannons were situated there.

And on that day the Ṣārī 'Askar asked the Shaykhs about the Mawlid al-Nabawī (the Prophet's Birthday) and why they had not started preparing the implements and requirements as usual. So Shaykh al-Bakrī excused himself, saying that the situation was stagnant (at present) and that funds were lacking. However the Ṣārī 'Askar did not accept this (excuse) and replied 'This must be done', and thereupon provided Shaykh al-Bakrī with three hundred *riyāl faransa* to help. So Shaykh al-Bakrī erected poles and set up ropes for the lamps. In the same manner the Ṣārī 'Askar set up many poles and ropes for lamps out of his own funds, in front of his house, and when Thursday arrived, which was the Yawm al-Mawlid, the Ṣārī 'Askar sent his band of drummers to the house of al-Bakrī, beating their drums throughout the day. All the French soldiers were present and did their drills from just before evening until sunset. Shaykh al-Bakrī invited the Ṣārī 'Askar, who came to his house and dined there, with his senior officers. After dinner, they went down to the house of the Ṣārī 'Askar with about fifty torchbearers preceding them. When the Ṣārī 'Askar reached his house, they displayed before him fire-crackers, fireworks (*ḥarāqat bārūd wa-nufūṭ*), and rockets which shot into the air, and fired cannons and the like for a good part of the night.

On that day, the Ṣārī 'Askar attired the Shaykh in a garment of furs and appointed him Naqīb al-Ashrāf (Head of the descendants of the Prophet), and this was proclaimed in the presence of the Wālī of Cairo. In addition it was proclaimed that he who has a claim against a Sharīf or a Sharīf against him must go to the house of the Naqīb al-Ashrāf.

And on that day news arrived that Ibrāhīm Bey and those who were with him had established themselves in Gaza.

On the fifteenth a great number of French soldiers set out southward, among them a senior officer who was placed in charge of Dajirjā and the Mu'allim (Master) Ya'qūb al-Qubṭī, the secretary of Sulaymān Bey who was to manage their affairs, show them the way, and devise for them all types of traps and deceptions. For example, when they sent a group of Europeans demanding taxes or the like he would have two or three of them change their attire and have them dress like Ottomans. He included in his letters to the populace a warning against disobedience since this was an Imperial decree. So these ruses deceived many of the country-folk and they would obey the orders.

And on that day the messenger whom the French had sent with a letter and a present to Aḥmad Pasha al-Jazzār in Acre arrived, this being when they had settled in Cairo. The messenger was accompanied by two or three Shāmī Christians in the capacity of merchants bearing a quantity of rice. The story that spread about them was that they disembarked from the port of Damietta on one of Aḥmad Pasha's ships and when they arrived at Acre and Aḥmad Pasha learned of this, he ordered that the European messenger be transferred to one of the corvettes (*naqāyir*) and would neither grant him audience nor accept anything from him, and ordered him to return. However, he detained the Shāmī Christians who came with him.

On the same day a group of Europeans arrived at the house of Riḍwān Kāshif al-Sha'rāwī accompanied by an architect. His wife was alarmed by them, because a few days previously she had made a settlement for her house and for her person at a sum of one thousand and three hundred *riyāls*, taking a letter (of confirmation to this effect) and sticking it to the door of her house. She had just brought back the property which she had kept (hidden) in various places and felt at ease once more. So when this group came to her she asked them 'What do you want now that I have already paid in full the agreed sum?'. They answered her 'It has reached us that you have in your possession arms and clothing belonging to the Mamlūks'. She denied this, so they said 'We will search'. She answered 'Search'. So they searched and went up to a place and discovered a secret chamber wherein they found twenty-four *shalwārs* (Turkish baggy trousers) of the costume of the Ghuzz, as well as *yeleks* (long vests), household goods, and the like. Under the first hiding-place they found another which contained many weapons, rifles, pistols and crates of gunpowder and the like. So they removed all these. Then they went underneath the stairs and dug up the earth and extracted two copper pots and a leather bag all filled with *riyāls farānsa* and a gold container inside which were gold *dīnārs*, all of which they removed. Then they went upstairs and brought the landlady down who was accompanied by a white slave girl. They took both of them together with their black slave girls bringing them to the house of the Qā'im Maqām, where she spent three nights. They robbed her of whatever / property, furnishings, and the like they found. They then imposed upon her (a further fine of) four thousand *riyāls* which she paid to them and then they freed her. So she returned to her house.

Because of this event they intensified the search for weapons and announced this publicly and also that they would search the houses after three days and kill anyone found in possession of weapons. As a result the people were frightened of these searches and said 'This is a trick designed merely for robbing the houses'. Afterwards they stopped it.

On the twentieth of that month it was agreed unanimously that Muṣṭafā Aghā, who was the Katkhudā 'l-Bāshā should be invested as Amīr al-Ḥajj. He presented himself at the house of the Qāḍī and was invested there in the presence of the Shaykhs. Moreover, the Ṣārī 'Askar took upon himself the obligation of expediting the requirements of the Ḥajj and of constructing a new *maḥmal* and other matters.

And on that day the Shaykhs asked that they receive their salaries from the Mint. They had requested this previously a number of times and the French had promised it to them over and over again. This time the interpreter told them 'Write up a list informing us of what is allotted to you'. So they wrote up a list, and what was allotted to them and to some others, came to about one thousand *fiḍḍas* (*para*) daily. When they had examined the list and had promised to fulfil its requirements several times, they said to them 'This time we shall give you instead *iltizām* (the right to collect taxes for a commission)'. But they replied 'So what are we going to do with this tax business when we all have different portions? Among us there are some who have fifty *fiḍḍas*, some thirty, and others twenty'. So the French replied 'Let one of you take charge of the matter, collect the money, and distribute it among his colleagues annually'. However, the Shaykhs did not accept this. So finally they shunned the whole matter, being convinced of the miserliness of the French in this matter. Before the French came, the salaries (*murattabāt*) were more than thirty-two thousand *fiḍḍas* daily.

On that day the holders of shares (of *iltizām*) asked for a renewal of their *iltizām* over the *taṣarruf* lands,[69] and in return the French demanded payment of the usual advance (*ḥulwān*) exceeding the stipulation of the law. However, they refused. So the French promised them that this would be dealt with after they had completed the recording and registration of the shares. They said 'Let anyone who has a tax-farming concession and whose legal deed (*taqsīṭ*)[70] is valid produce it and register it'. So within a number of days they acted accordingly but matters remained as they were.

And on that day the French levied taxes including *kulaf* (impost for the upkeep of the military) and *tafārīd* (appointed taxes) of the country and issued edicts to this effect in which they stated that the above should be deduced from the total imposts of tax land (*al-māl*). In implementation of this they appointed tax collectors (*ṣarrāfs*) from among the Copts who went into the country like rulers wreaking havoc among the Muslims with arrests, beatings, insults, and ceaseless harassment in their demands for money. Furthermore they terrorized them with threats of bringing in the French soldiers if they did not pay up the determined amount quickly; all this occurred by means of Coptic planning and trickery.

On Thursday the twenty-fifth of the month, the French killed a Sharīf (descendant of Muḥammad) in al-Rumayla, an inhabitant of Alexandria, called al-Sayyid Muḥammad Kurayyim.[71] And the story of this executed man is that he was a public weigher (*qabbānī*) who weighed goods with a steelyard at a shop situated in the port. He was very agile of movement and friendly in social relations, ceaselessly endearing himself to people by virtue of his friendly disposition. He also sought to satisfy the civil servants and others, such as Muslim and Christian merchants, in addition to the notables among his own people. In this way he gained the love of the people and became famous and well known in the ports of Alexandria and Rosetta and Cairo. He became close to Ṣāliḥ Bey when the latter was the deputy (*wakīl*) of Dār al-Sa'āda (the House of Felicity — the Porte) at the time when his word was influential in the port of Rosetta but not in Alexandria, so that he made Rosetta and its suburbs as if they were his own tax concession *(iltizām)* and he ruled in it as he wished and appointed a Greek from Crete called 'Uthmān Khojā who ruled arbitrarily and devised all sorts of ways to seize and confiscate the property of its people, and he brought wealth to his lord by all possible tricks. So this above-mentioned Sayyid Muḥammad came to an accord with him and through him and others reached Ṣāliḥ Bey and through the latter also Murād Bey. Consequently he entered his confidence concerning matters relating to the port and came into his favour. This man was suitable to the aims which Murād Bey desired — because the port of Alexandria was respected and its people were united and in complete agreement. For this reason the orders that came from the Amīrs in Cairo had no influence and they could not rule freely in Alexandria as they did in other places and they could not confiscate money or property from any one of its inhabitants. The Sirdār (commander-in-chief) who was appointed by the Amīrs, as well as the Mu'allim (Master) of the Dīwān, could only act within the confines of the established laws.

Among the inhabitants of Alexandria dwelt a *faqīh* (Muslim jurist) of the Mālikīs called Shaykh Muḥammad al-Masīrī who gave them lessons and explained *fiqh* (the theory and practice of jurisprudence) to them according to the Imām Mālik, showing no interest in what they owned, refraining from committing any act which would raise suspicion, and avoiding what was forbidden, and their hearts united in love for him and they devoted themselves to obeying him in such a way that he became an authority for them in all matters. When a problem confronted them suddenly, they would hasten to him and put it before him awaiting his opinion on the particular matter at hand. And they would heed his word and the view that he had expressed. Whatever he ordered they would obey and whatever he prohibited they would avoid. Whenever one of the rulers or others / wished to interfere with the life of even the lowliest of them in an unlawful manner, and when the people informed this *faqīh* about it he would hand down a decision, and they would all hasten together to the violator and might even beat him up and they would expel him from among them. The Amīrs of Cairo had concealed their hatred for the people of the port and this man, awaiting an opportunity to achieve their desires and disrupt the unity that was in the hearts of the people until the aforementioned Sayyid Muḥammad appeared and made contact with Ṣāliḥ Bey and Murād Bey and their adjutants. He became close to them and as a result they raised him above his companions with regard to his status, and put him in charge of the Dīwān and the Gamārik (customs-house) of the port. As a result his status rose and his word became powerful and he came to be the most influential in the management of affairs. He increased the duties and customs and became very crafty in confiscating goods especially with regard to European merchants, whom he singled out in particular when it came to increasing the duties to be paid on their merchandise. After he had collected what taxes he had imposed he would send to Murād Bey and inform him of what merchandise had arrived, such as broadcloth (*jūkh*) and the like and tell him where it was situated and that such and such merchandise was on the way to Cairo aboard such and such a ship. Then Murād Bey would send someone to watch for the arrival of the ship and take whatever he wanted from the ship itself or from the storehouses at the price in the merchants' register but without paying. The Amīrs of Murād Bey followed his example. It also

Sultan Hassan Mosque of Cairo

happened that a European ship arrived in which there were a number of barrels containing a great quantity of Venetian gold all of which the above-mentioned Sayyid Muḥammad took, and sent to Murād Bey.

All these dealings were one of the most important reasons for the French military action, this action which spread over us and infested us. In the previous year the above-mentioned Sayyid Muḥammad went to Cairo intending to set out on the Ḥajj, and the highest as well as the lowest welcomed him with celebrations and festivities, presenting him with gifts and escorting him a great length of the way. Similarly when he returned by way of al-Qulzum (the Red Sea) the people awaited him expectantly for several days in the tents of the bedouin. Some even set out each day and came back. When he reached the tents of the bedouin, Ṣāliḥ Bey and many notables went out to meet him and also the notables of Alexandria and Rosetta and all of them met him there and returned to Cairo with him riding on a nimble mule which was given to him, riding beside the mount of Ṣāliḥ Bey, and they received him and set him up in large house. In addition presents and gifts were bestowed upon him. He himself filled many bundles and packs with all kinds of cloths which he brought with him from the Ḥijāz to Murād Bey, Ṣāliḥ Bey, Muḥammad Bey al-Alfī, Ibrāhīm Katkhudā al-Sinnārī, and other eminent merchants, famous people, and notables, each person according to his station. When he went to greet Murād Bey he bestowed upon him a valuable fur of sable and he also brought a fur garment and a long piece of cloth which he had purchased for him at a price of one thousand *riyāls*. Then he returned to the city of Alexandria, and once he set his foot there he began to raise a sum of money to send to Murād Bey. The first thing he did was to have Sayyid Aḥmad Abū Shuhba, the Naqīb al-Ashrāf and his deputy in the Diwān, come before him and give an account of his income and expenditure and (found) that a sum of money due to him from his deputy was late in coming, for the above-mentioned Sayyid Aḥmad was benevolent toward the people and treated them kindly in matters of customs and duties, and it happened that twenty sacks containing raw silk arrived at the port destined for a certain merchant, but the deputy registered them in the register as four sacks of silk and sixteen of broad beans. Sayyid Muḥammad was informed of this matter and asked Sayyid Aḥmad about it. He replied 'There was nothing other than what was recorded'. Sayyid Muḥammad went to the warehouse of this merchant and removed the sacks of silk and denounced Sayyid Aḥmad and forced him to pay the customs (*maks*) on the sacks. He also demanded that he should pay for the discrepancy in the former account and dealt severely with him; as a result the quarrelling and tension between them mounted, and Shaykh al-Masīrī, to whom the people of the port turned, took his side, so the people split into three factions, one of them behind Sayyid Muḥammad Kurayyim, another with al-Masīrī and Abū Shuhba, backing truth, and yet another renouncing both sides out of fear of the consequences. However, the majority were behind Sayyid Muḥammad. The latter sent to his master (*makhdūm*) complaining about the people of the port, asking him to send a *kāshif* (a sub-provincial governor) who would strengthen him and give him support. The people then mediated between them and brought them to reconciliation. However, Sayyid Muḥammad was unable to prevent his request from being fulfilled. Immediately afterward Murād Bey sent Ḥasan Aghā his former *khāzin dār* (treasurer), a cunning man, and he reached the port. /Abū Shuhba knew that he would be the first to be called; his fear increased and he felt anxious, so he went into hiding. He was looked for but he was not to be found. Some days later he was found dead in the cistern of his house. Then they took everything they found there and revised the accounts in which Abū Shuhba had reduced the (expected) income or those with which he had tampered, and collected it from those people.

Then the plague spread in the port until Ḥasan Agha died of it. Thus the days passed one after another and the French troops arrived and took possession of the port. They arrested the above-mentioned Sayyid Muḥammad Kurayyim and demanded that he return the money and harassed him. Then they imprisoned him in a ship. When they reached Cairo and entered the palace of Murād Bey they also found in his meeting room (*majlis*) Muḥammad's letters with information about them urging and inciting Murād Bey to fight them and disparaging them. So they became furious with him and had him brought to Cairo where he was imprisoned in the (house) of the Qā'im Maqām (the Governor of Cairo). Then the Shaykhs of the Dīwān went to intercede several times, but the French answered them with procrastination. They then asked that he might be transferred to the keeping of one of them, but the French would not allow this until, on the above-mentioned Wednesday evening, Magallon, the greatest criminal of them all, came to him and said to him 'What is demanded from you is such and such a sum'. He gave him a respite of twelve hours, telling him that he would be executed if he had not paid by the time this period expired. The next morning (Sayyid Muḥammad) sent to the Shaykhs begging that they help him. So some of them came to him, in the company of Sayyid Aḥmad al-Maḥrūqī, the head of the merchants (*kabīr al-tujjār*) and others to whom he pleaded and begged, seeking their help, crying out 'Ransom my life, O Muslims'. But they had not the means at hand to ransom him, for everyone was preoccupied with himself expecting that some evil might fall on his own head. So they dispersed, leaving him to himself. And just before noon when the period of respite expired they brought him down and set him upon an ass, several soldiers holding unsheathed swords surrounding him, beating a drum in front of them. So they passed through al-Ṣalība his hands tied behind his back, until they reached al-Rumayla. Then they tied him with his arms stretched out and fired upon him with rifles as was their practice with those whom they executed. Then they decapitated him, raising his head on a quarter-staff. Then they rode about al-Rumayla with it while the town-crier proclaimed 'This is the punishment of those who disobey the French'. Afterwards his slaves took his head and buried it with his body. Thus his story ends, and this day coincided with that of the year before in which he rode in great pomp and splendour, when he was entering Cairo, returning from the Ḥijāz as was mentioned above when the people shouted while he was riding with the Amīrs and notables surrounding him — and behind him those who came out to receive him together with his *mamlūks* and black slaves — 'Praised be the Munificent, the Generous'. And on the day of his execution 'Praised be He who raises and debases'.[72] Indeed the wise man is he who is content with what God has granted him of worldly things and who is satisfied with a small portion and who lives securely in obscurity and does not meddle in affairs and who clings only to his Lord and who avoids anybody except Him.

On that day the members of the Dīwān went to the head of the Dīwān and they were invited to go to the Ṣārī 'Askar. Shaykh al-Sharqāwī, al-Ṣāwī, and those who were present went to him. After sitting for a while, the Ṣārī 'Askar got up from his seat and brought a three-piece *ṭaylasān* (a shawl-like garment) of red, white, and blue and put it on Shaykh al-Sharqāwī's shoulder. The latter removed it with his hand and put it on the floor, asking to be excused from wearing it. The interpreter said 'Oh Shaykhs! You have become dear friends of the Ṣārī 'Askar, and his intention is to glorify you and to honour you with his attire and token, because if you are thus marked, the soldiers and the people will extol you and you will fill a great place in their hearts. They answered 'But our esteem may fail in the eyes of our Muslim brothers'. The Ṣārī 'Askar became angry with Shaykh al-Sharqāwī and said 'This man is unsuited for leadership' and some other words in his own language which have the same meaning. The rest of the group treated them politely and asked to be excused from wearing this shawl. The interpreter said 'If you don't do this, you must put the emblem *(al-'alāma)* on your breast'. They answered 'Grant us time to think it over', and they agreed on a respite of twelve days. Meanwhile Shaykh al-Sādāt arrived, answering an official summons. He met them while they were leaving. After sitting for a while, the Ṣārī 'Askar began to flatter him with pleasantries which were translated by the interpreter, laughing and kissing his hand at times, his knee at others, displaying affection and friendship. He presented a jewelled ring to him and asked him to come the following day. He left with great honour. On that day the corps of the guards (*qulluqāt*) called on the people to wear the emblems, known as the rose (*warda*), which consists of three circles of cloth or something else, joined together in three colours, blue, white, and red, about as big as the curve of the palm. The circles are of diminishing sizes. The second is smaller than the first and the third is smaller than the second in such a way that the three colours remain distinct. They sometimes fringed the edges of the circles and embellished it, and they were versatile in decorating it. It signifies obedience and submission and among them it is a sign of affection. The people became clamorous and most of them crowded to the tailors. Snips which were in accordance with these colours found a good market. But there were others who disdained that and found it repulsive. During the evening of that day they announced that (the wearing of) it should be abolished among the common people.

On the morning of that day Shaykh al-Sādāt visited the Ṣārī 'Askar. The latter greeted him and made some overtures to the former to wear the emblem. Because of the good nature of the Shaykh he complied with him and did not decline. He was very pleased with this and brought a rose (of the three colours) and pinned it with a fine pin on the garment of the Shaykh who smiled at him, and the other was very happy. The rest of the Shaykhs arrived, and the Shaykh and the interpreter told them 'You also oblige the Ṣārī 'Askar and don't oppose him in pinning on the rose, and when you leave, remove it'. So they said nothing. The Ṣārī 'Askar got up and pinned a rose on everyone while they were expressing contentment and he was happy with that. They were unable to refuse, especially when they saw the rose in the garment of the Shaykh. When the party was finished and they left his presence they removed it from their garments. Later on they used to put it on when they entered his reception room and when they left they removed it, and thus was their situation.

At the end of that month the French began to prepare for their feast at Birkat al-Azbakiyya. That is because when they killed their Sultan, and their republic was proclaimed according to the order they invented and the rule which they created, as was mentioned before, they made that day the beginning of their calendar and a feast. This day corresponds to the autumn equinox, in which the sun enters the *Domicilium* of Libra. They started to transport wood and to dig many pits. They brought an extremely large and thick pole, dug a big pit for it, lined the inside of it with mud and stone, and around it piled great quantities of earth. They erected that pole in its centre with instruments and shear-legs (*maqaṣṣāt*)[73] of wood, pulleys with gauges and ropes. They constructed upon the pole a wooden form pointed at the top with a square base. They covered its remaining part from top to bottom with thick cloth and painted it with paint similar to plaster. At its lower part there was a base in which there were drawings in black and white. Opposite Bāb al-Hawā in the Birka (pool) they also made a structure in the shape of a great gate of lattice-work wood. They covered it with a painted cloth like the one mentioned before, and the upper part of the basket was painted in white with drawings in black representing their soldiers fighting the Egyptians. Parallel to it, in the direction of the vaulted bridge from which the water enters the Birka there was another gate which was different in shape from the first designated for fireworks (*ḥarāqat bārūd*). They erected many wooden poles from that gate to the other, like a wide circle which surrounded most of the Birka, in such a way that the big pole was situated in the centre. Between these poles, they stretched ropes. They also suspended on them two rows of lamps and lamps arranged in the likeness of various figures (*tamāthīl*)[74] between the poles and the fireworks. They accomplished all this in a few days.

The month of Rabī al-Thānī

This month started on a Wednesday, on which day the news arrived that when the Ghuzz of Upper Egypt, that is, Murād Bey and his company, heard that the French were approaching, they retreated in the direction of al-Fayyūm, while ʻUthmān Bey al-Ashqar crossed to the eastern bank and went to his master (*sayyid*) from behind the mountain to Gaza. A group of French soldiers went out eastward with / several camels and loads. The Ghuzz and the bedouin, who were with them, attacked them and took from them several camels with their loads but the French did not pursue them.

On the third of the month a letter directed to the Shaykhs and others arrived from Ibrāhīm Bey, saying 'You have to be calm and safeguard yourselves and the people. His Majesty the Sultan sent soldiers to us from land and sea; God willing, we shall soon come to you'. When this message arrived, the Ṣārī ʻAskar enquired about it, so it was sent to him and read in his presence, he said 'The Mamlūks are liars'. It

Cairo, view from outside the city walls

happened also that an Aghā Bishlī[75] (Aghā of the light cavalry) arrived from Alexandria, and excitement and clamour spread among the people all that day. They said 'An Aghā came to us from the Sulṭān'. Others said 'This is an ambassador (envoy, elchi) who usually comes with the squadron (*dūnānma*) and the naval fleet (*'imāra*) in which the soldiers and the fighting forces come'. It happened that day also that the Ṣārī 'Askar came to Shaykh al-Sādāt in his house, which is in the vicinity of al-Mashhad al-Ḥusaynī. He sat with him for a while and then returned. A mob of people assembled in the Ḥusaynī Mosque, and their clamour increased. Some of them said 'Here he came to the Shaykh for fear that the people would revolt'. Some others said 'He came at this time in order that the Shaykh would get safe-conduct for him'. Others said 'He came in order to embrace Islam for fear of his life', and similar speculations. When he was riding back, and they saw him passing the gate of the Ḥusaynī Mosque, they all called out with one voice, reciting the *Fātiḥa*. He and his soldiers were astonished by their clamour and tumult. Later on, it was clear that this Bishlī had arrived forty days earlier carrying correspondence from the Vizier directed to 'Ali Bey, the Qābujī Bāshā (first chamberlain) who was appointed to the collection of the *māl* (revenue of the Imperial Treasury) and *khazna* (tribute). The Europeans isolated him on the ship in Alexandria with the passengers for fear that the plague had infected them. When forty days had passed, they disembarked them and gave them permission to travel after they had suffered badly from the confinement and anguish as well as the smoke which was used to disinfect them inside the hold, that is to say, the interior of the ship. This was in addition to the high prices and so on.

On that day, they began to remove the gates, and (those of the) cul-de-sacs also, and to transport them to Birkat al-Azbakiyya, because most of the gates had been transported and thrown there. Those gates which they were not able to remove, were cut into halves and removed to the Birka. The people thought that the wood was to be used to build a structure in order to commemorate their feast day, but the French did not do anything with the wood and they (the former gates) remained thrown all along the pavement of the Raṣīf al-Khashshāb up to the middle of the Birka.

Saturday, the eleventh of that month, was their appointed feast day. That morning, they fired several cannons and they placed upon every wooden pole one of their coloured *bandiera*. They beat their drums and their soldiers assembled in the Birka, the cavalry, the infantry, and the carabineers. The Shaykhs, the grandees, the Copts, and the Shāmīs arrived at the house of their eminent chief, the Ṣārī 'Askar, and sat there part of the day. The Copts attired themselves with their most splendid garments. Jirjis al-Jawharī, the chief of the Copts, wore a *kurka* (a fur garment) similar to the full-dress of the viziers, embroidered with filigree (*qaṣab*) from the shoulders to the cuffs. Also along the front of the garment were embroidered sun-like ornaments (*shamsāt*) of filigree with buttons. Philotheos wore a long-sleeved robe (*farajiyya*) embroidered with filigree along its sleeves and front. All of them wore cashmere turbans, rode on agile mules, and expressed great joy on that day. Then the French dignitaries accompanied by the Shaykhs, the Qāḍī and the *katkhudā* (deputy) of the Pasha descended to the great pole. Then they spread out large carpets on the high ground at the foot of the pole. The soldiers began their military exercises displaying their war manœuvres with guns and cannons. After they finished, the soldiers assembled in rows around the pole and a document was read to them in their language which was translated by someone in the audience. It stated briefly: 'We inform the soldiers that we arrived in Egypt, captured it and killed the Mamlūks who inhabited it and by God's will after the end of the feast, we will set out against the rest and kill them and you shall return to your country. In your place others will come to inhabit this country'. / Afterwards, they got up and the gathering dispersed. The Ṣārī 'Askar returned to his home, accompanied by the members of the Dīwān, such as the Shaykhs and others. He prepared a sumptuous dinner for them. They ate and left. At sunset they lit all the lamps which were hanging on the ropes, as well as those arranged in the likeness of various figures and chandeliers of six lamps (*aḥmāl*)[76] on the houses. In the evening they had a display of fire crackers, rockets (*ṣawārīkh*), fireworks (*nufūṭ*), like wheels and water mills of fire (*shibh sawāqī wa-dawālīb min nār*), and several cannonades, which lasted two hours. The lamps remained lit until daylight. Then they undid the ropes, the suspended chandeliers (*ta'ālīq*)[77] and the lamps arranged in the likeness of various figures (*tamāthīl*). The gate which was opposite to Bāb al-Hawā remained as did also the big pole underneath which a group of soldiers kept watch day and night because of its significance as an emblem, a symbol of the existence of their state, and a distinguished mark of their country — may God hasten its end.

On the second night of this month the Ṣārī 'Askar rode to the bank

Three great sheiks of Cairo (Paintings by Rigo)
Sheik El Cherkaouy, Sheik El Fayoumy, Moallem El Geoari

of al-Jīza and sent soldiers to the region in which Murād Bey was, and other soldiers to the Sharqiyya region with cannons on wheels.[78] On the same day, the Qā'im Maqām, Dupuy, sent designated people to Sit Nafīsa, asking for the wife of 'Uthmān Bey al-Jūkhadār (*Çoḳadār* 'Valet'). So she appealed to the Shaykhs for help. The Shaykh al-Mahdī and Shaykh al-Sirsī arrived and tried to prevent her (from going) but they were unable. So they accompanied her and dealt with her affair. The reason for her being summoned was that they had found a servant (*farrāsh*) in possession of some tobacco and clothes. They arrested him and interrogated him. He informed them that he was her slave (*tābi'*) and that she had given him these things and had made an arrangement for him to return once more in order to take two chibouks (*shubbuk*) of tobacco, a fur, and five hundred *maḥbūbs* which were to be delivered to his patron. This was the reason for her being called in. They said 'And where is the servant?', and sent someone to bring him. They interrogated her but she denied everything completely. They waited for the arrival of the servant until after sunset but he didn't come. So the Shaykhs said to the French 'Let her return home and tomorrow we will come and investigate this affair'. Dupuy said 'Non, non'. The Shaykhs said 'Let her go and we will sleep here in her place'. He refused that too, and they defended her as well as they could. When they gave up all hope, they left her and went. She spent the night in a part of the house and with her were a group of Muslim and European women. Next morning the Shaykhs rode with the Katkhudā 'l-Bāshā and the Qāḍī. They rode together and went to the Ṣārī 'Askar. The latter had her brought to him and handed her to the Qāḍī, but they could not prove anything against her in this groundless case, (still) they imposed upon her (a fine), the sum of three thousand *riyāl farānsa*. So she went to one of her houses adjacent to the Qāḍī's and dwelled there.

On Monday they declared in the markets that everyone who had a mule had to take it to the house of the Qā'im Maqām in Birkat al-Fīl, and receive its value. If the mule was not brought voluntarily, it would be taken by force and the owner would have to pay three hundred *riyāls farānsa*. If the mule was brought voluntarily, the owner would receive fifty *riyāls*, whether its value was more or less. The owners of bad mules profited while the owners of valuable mules lost. Afterwards this was stopped.

That same day they also announced that lamps should be lit all night in the streets and markets. Each house was required to have a lamp as well as every third shop. The people were to sweep, splash water, and clean the streets of the rubbish, filth, and dead cats. This was in spite of the fact that the streets and houses where the French lived, were full of filth, infected earth mixed with bird feathers, the entrails of animals, garbage, the stench of their drinks, the sourness of their alcoholic beverages, their urine and excrement, such that a passer-by was obliged to hold his nose.

That same day they ordered all foreigners, such as the Maghribīs and others and unemployed servants, to return to their countries. And anyone who was found to remain would deserve his punishment. After they repeated the proclamation and gave a respite of twenty-four hours, a group of Maghribīs went to the Ṣārī 'Askar and said: 'Show us a road so that we can go because the land route is impassable and the

English are blocking / the sea, preventing travellers from leaving. Nor are we able to live in Alexandria because of the high prices and the lack of water there', so he let them stay.

On that day they appointed Ibrāhīm al-Mi'mār the Aghā[79] of the Mutafarriqa Qabṭān al-Suways (captain of Suez),[80] and some soldiers accompanied him with a French flag. The bedouin attacked them and robbed them and killed the above-mentioned Ibrāhīm Aghā and those who were in his company and only a few escaped.

At that time interest dwindled in the Dīwān to which the Shaykhs used to go at the (residence of the) Amīr of the Dīwān in the house of Qāyit Aghā. They had attended it for several days but nobody came, so they went home and stayed there. Then they stopped going and nobody asked for them.

On that day they set up a new Dīwān which they called the Court of Cases (*Maḥkamat al-Qaḍāyā*). To this effect they issued a decree (*firmān*) in which they included clauses in a style revolting to one's nature and disgusting to one's ear. They appointed six Copts and six Muslim merchants to the Dīwān. Malaṭī the Copt, who had previously acted as secretary to Ayyūb Bey, the Daftardār was appointed as its head and Qāḍī. To this Dīwān the French assigned the handling of cases involving commercial and civil affairs, inheritances, and lawsuits. In the form of this Dīwān the French established a basis for malice, a foundation for godlessness, a bulwark of injustice, and a source of all manner of evil innovations. The French had a large roll written concerning the new Dīwān and sent copies of it to the notables. Other copies were posted at crossroads, at entrances to lanes, and on the doors of the mosques. Within the text they inserted stipulations and in their contents were others. These were substipulations formulated in their stupid idiom and crude style, and all of them dedicated to one purpose, namely robbing people of their money by devious means and despoiling them of their real estate, inherited property and the like. Among these stipulations, which can only be understood after much pondering on the meaning of their expressions was that property-owners must bring their certificates (*ḥujja*) and title-deeds (*tamassuk*) as their evidence of their right of possession. However, when deeds were brought forward, showing the basis of ownership whether by virtue of sale or their — say inheritance, this was not considered sufficient. The property-owners were then ordered to look up their particular title-deeds in the registers, a service for which they had to pay a sum of money stated in that roll.

If a landowner's title-deed was found in the register, confirmation was demanded from him; upon bringing proof by legal evidence and upon this being accepted by the authorities the landowner had to pay another fee in return for this evidence and an official document of possession (*tamkīn*) was written out for him. An investiture would then be drawn up for him after which they assessed its value. The landlord then had to pay two per cent. If it happened that the landlord had no certificate, or if he had one and it was not recorded in the register, or recorded and that record was not confirmed, then his holdings would be confiscated by the Dīwān of the Republic (*Dīwān al-Jumhūr*) and became its property. This was one of the most malicious artifices by which the French stripped owners of their holdings and lands, since people acquire their property either by purchase or by inheritance in the form of a new certificate (*ḥujja*) or an old one or through a similar document from their forefathers. In many cases it was difficult or impossible for a landowner to prove the validity of his certificate and verify its existence in the registers due to incidents of death or travel. In other cases witnesses did come forward but were not accepted by the authorities. If it happened that they were accepted, the French treated them as mentioned above.

Taxes on inheritances and death duties were among the taxes collected, in sums of varying amounts. As for death duties, the relatives of the deceased had to announce his death and pay a sum for this announcement and open succession within twenty-four hours. If more than twenty-four hours passed, his estate would be confiscated for the Dīwān and the heirs would forfeit their rights. However, if the opening of succession was not delayed but opened according to the regulation with the permission of the Dīwān, a direct tax had to be paid. The same applied to the proof of the status of heir, then after receiving their shares the heirs were to pay a direct tax but with a substantial addition. Similarly, if someone had a claim of debt against the deceased, he had to prove it before the Dīwān of the *Ḥashriyyāt*,[81] had to pay a fee, and get a receipt with which he could collect his debt. Upon collecting his debt he had to pay the surplus tax. Like measures were applied in the farming of taxes (*iltizām*), the *rizaq* (land for religious endowment), and cultivated lands (*aṭyān*), with all manner of stipulations and conditions as well as on deeds of gift (*hibāt*), sales (*mabī'āt*), pleas (*da'āwā*), disputes (*munāza'āt*), quarrels (*mushājarāt*), and written certifications (*ishhādāt*) of minor and major matters. / One also could not travel

Mosque of Sultan Hassan in Cairo, interior view (Engraving by Dutertre)

without a permit (*waraqa*) for which one had to pay a fee. Also a tax was levied on births. It was called attestation of existence *(ithbāt al-ḥayāt)*. Similarly with regard to leases and the receipt of rents for properties (*al-mu'ājarāt wa-qabḍ ujar al-amlāk*) and so on. May the omnipotent, the Doer in His omnipotence not allow them to be realized.

On the same day the police (*aṣḥāb al-darak*) called upon the public to desist from meddling in and discussing political matters, or if a group of wounded or defeated soldiers passed their way, not to mock them or clap, as they habitually did.

And on that day the French looted the property of the soldiers of the galleon who had served the Amīrs. They also plundered the caravanserai of 'Alī Bey which was situated on the bank of the Būlāq and another at al-Jamāliyya, seizing their wares and those of their partners, on the pretext that they had fought against them on the side of the Mamlūks, and escaped with them (the Mamlūks).

On that day they seized Muḥammad Katkhudā Abū Sayf who was Sirdār in Damietta appointed by the Amīrs. Formerly he had acted as a Katkhudā to Ḥasan Bey al-Jaddāwī.[82] Once he arrived they imprisoned him in the Citadel. With him they also imprisoned a servant (*farrāsh*) of Ibrāhīm Bey.

On that day they ordered the inhabitants of the Citadel to vacate their homes and move into town and live there. Thus the inhabitants left the Citadel and the French brought up cannons which they positioned in various places. They further demolished some buildings and erected walls. Thus they pulled down the high places and raised up the low places. They built on the foundations of Bāb al-'Azab in al-Rumayla and changed its features and disfigured its beauties and wiped out the monuments of scholars and the assembly rooms of sultans and great men and took what works of art were left on its great gates and in its magnificent sitting-rooms (*iywān*) such as arms, shields, axes, helmets, and Indian lances and balls with chains of the warriors (*ukar al-fidāwiyya*).[83] They demolished the palace of Yūsuf Ṣalāḥ al-Dīn and the council halls of kings and sultans which had high supports and tall pillars, as well as the mosques and chapels (*zawāyā*) of religious orders and shrines. They disfigured the Great Mosque, the lofty distinguished one which was built by the man of glorious deeds, Muḥammad ibn Qalāwūn al-Malik al-Nāṣir. They removed its *minbar* (pulpit), wrecked its *iywān*, took its wood, shook its pillars, and removed its iron stool near its praying area (*maqṣūra*) a wondrously wrought work in which the Sultan used to pray. Thus they behaved as the enemies of the Religion would behave but 'Our trust is in God alone, and He is an excellent protector'.

On that day, a great number of troops went for Murād Bey at Baḥr Yūsuf.

On Thursday the sixteenth it was [proclaimed] that if anyone had a quarrel with a Christian or a Jew, or vice versa, one antagonist could testify against the other, and demand for him to be brought to the house of the Ṣārī 'Askar.

On that day they killed two persons and walked around with their heads, calling out 'This is the punishment of all who deliver letters from the Mamlūks or bring letters to them'.

On that day they told the people to desist from burying the dead in cemeteries close to dwellings, such as the cemeteries of al-Azbakiyya and al-Ruway'ī and to bury them only in graveyards far (from the populated areas). Those who had no vaults in the cemetery should bury their dead in the vaults of the Mamlūks. And when they buried someone they were required to increase the depth of the graves. They further ordered people to hang out their clothing, furnishings, and bedding on their roofs for several days and to fumigate their houses with fumes which would remove the putrescence. All this was out of fear, as they claimed, of the smell and contagion of the plague. The French said that the putrescence is imprisoned in the depths of the earth. When winter sets in and the depths of the earth become cold because of the flow of the Nile, the rain, and the dampness, what is imprisoned in the earth comes out with its rotten vapours and the air becomes rotten, so epidemic and plague occur.

As for the French it is their custom not to bury their dead but to toss them on garbage heaps like the corpses of dogs and beasts, or to throw them into the sea. Among the other things which they said is that when someone becomes sick they must inform the French who then send an authorized representative to examine him and to find out whether he has the plague or not. Then they decide what to do with him.

On Saturday the eighteenth a group of guards (*qawwāsa*) in the service of the French started to demolish the monuments set up on the graves in the al-Azbakiyya cemetery, levelling them to the ground. The news concerning this spread / and the owners of the vaults in this area heard of this one from the other. They came from all sides, most of them women who lived in the quarters of al-Madābigh, Kawm al-Shaykh Salāma, al-Fawwāla, al-Manāṣra, Qanṭarat Amīr Ḥusayn, and Qal'at al-Kilāb until they were like a swarm of locusts, crying out and clamouring. They gathered at al-Azbakiyya and stood before the house of the Ṣārī 'Askar. So the French sent to them interpreters who excused themselves saying that the Ṣārī 'Askar had no knowledge of this demolition and that he only ordered that the burial cease. Consequently they returned to where they came from and the demolition was halted.

On that day the French had the Shaykhs write a report to the Sultan and another to the Sharīf of Mekka. Then they printed a number of copies of these letters and posted them in the streets and at crossroads. The contents in brief after the regular usage in the preface were: 'To the Sharīf of Mekka, the Sharīf Ghālib, all other Sharīfs, the *'ulamā'*, and all the people', mentioning the arrival of the French and their battles with the Mamlūks and the flight of the latter, and that a group of the *'ulamā'* had gone to the French on the western bank and that he (Napoleon) had given them and the people *amān* excluding the Mamlūks and that he (Napoleon) had informed them that he was one of the intimate friends of the Sultan and the enemy of his enemies; further, that the minting of money, the Friday sermon in the name of the Sultan, and the rites of Islam were to remain in effect as they had always been. In addition, they mentioned other matters which they (the French) had mentioned in their former proclamation, such as their saying that they are Muslims and that they respect the Prophet and the Qur'ān, and that they had brought the pilgrims who were dispersed in various places together and treated them honourably, providing mounts for those who were on foot, feeding the hungry, and providing water for the thirsty. In addition they mentioned the fact that they had devoted their attention to the day of the Festival, that is the day of the Breaking of the Dam, with much celebration in order to make the believers happy, and that they had spent money in alms (*ṣadaqa*) for the poor. Similarly they mentioned in the letter that they had devoted much attention to the Holiday celebrating the Birth of the Prophet, spending money in organizing the celebrations on a magnificent scale for its greater glory.

'We and the French have agreed to invest the Most Honourable Muṣṭafā Aghā, the venerable Katkhudā of Bakr Pasha, as the present Wālī of Egypt and we have approved of this that the connection with the Ottoman Empire may remain'.

'In addition the French are making efforts to complete the provision of the requirements for the pilgrimage to the two Holy Places, Mekka and Medīna, and have ordered us to inform you of this, Etcetera, and that is all'. Under this were the signatures of the Shaykhs who wrote their names.

On Saturday, among the trivial events which occurred, was that a certain man, a money-changer by profession, who lived in the Jamāliyya district in the vicinity of the Jawwāniyya quarter, through a slip of the tongue said that 'Sayyid al-Badawī in the east and al-Dasūqī in the west were killing every Christian passing by'. Furthermore he uttered these words in the presence of Shāmī Christians. One of them answered back using nasty words and a fight broke out. So the Christian got up and went to Dupuy the Qā'im Maqām and told him the story. As a result he sent for the money-changer and put him under arrest. They nailed up his shop and sealed two houses belonging to him and imprisoned him. The Shaykhs intervened on his behalf a number of times until the French released him two days later and sent him to the house of al-Bakrī to be punished there, the alternative being the payment of five hundred [*riyāls*] *farānsa*. He received a hundred strokes of the lash and was freed. Similarly they released the remainder of those imprisoned.

On Monday they did the rounds of the various quarters and caravanserai and registered their names, and the names of their gatekeepers. They ordered them not to let any foreigner take up residence there nor to let anyone to travel except with the permission of the Aghā Mustaḥfaẓān.

On Tuesday they celebrated the Birthday of al-Ḥusayn which the Muslims had intended to abstain from this year. This happened because a certain hypocrite had engaged in intrigues among the French. It happened that a discussion had taken place about it being customary to celebrate the Birthday of al-Ḥusayn right after that of the Prophet and Bonaparte had asked why they did not do it and this hypocrite had said 'The intention of Shaykh al-Sādāt is to do it only when the Mamlūks return'. Shaykh al-Sādāt heard about this and started the celebrations but shortened them to a period of seven nights while formerly it was celebrated for fifteen nights, the last of them being on this above-mentioned Tuesday. The Ṣārī 'Askar appeared at the house of Shaykh al-Sādāt by invitation and dined there, afterwards riding home again.

And on that day the '*ulamā*' and the notables from Alexandria, Damietta, and the rest of the districts presented themselves by invitation to appear in the Dīwān which the French had instituted for the

Bonaparte presiding over the Cairo Divan (Engraving by Raffet)

purpose of establishing the (new) system which we have mentioned previously.

Also on that day a group of soldiers set out to reinforce those soldiers who had gone against Murād Bey.

On Thursday the twenty-third of this month news arrived that the soldiers who had set out against Murād Bey and his followers had met with them and exchanged fire with them for some time. Then the Mamlūks simulated flight, enticing the French troops to follow them to the foot of mount al-Lāhūn where they fell upon the French like the true men they were(?). / They fired at each other continuously. The Mamlūks arranged their soldiers in lines and set an ambush in their famous and well-tried way. When the two parties met and the firing continued from both sides and the dust rose among them and the face of the day darkened, then the lines of the Mamlūks took them by surprise with swords and caused them to taste death massacring them, slaughtering them, and leaving the greater part of them lying on the ground. Those that survived turned their backs and fled toward the sea seeking safety. At this point those lying in ambush rushed upon the French, cutting their throats and leaving the bodies on the ground. Those who escaped by swimming or fleeing encountered the bedouin who extirpated what remained of them, tackling them from every point, and rare indeed were those who escaped and thus those French went the way of all flesh. When the news spread and passed from ear to ear and became well known people rejoiced in their hearts and were delighted, seeing this as an omen of the beginning of the French defeat.

On that same day the great gate (triumphal arch) which the French had erected in Birkat al-Azbakiyya opposite Bāb al-Hawā (to commemorate their victory), collapsed and the people also took this as a good omen. The reason for the collapse was that when they prevented the water from entering the Birka and shut the dam, as was mentioned previously, the water filtered through the ground of the Birka with the result that it became soft and the gate collapsed.

On Friday they summoned the Shaykhs, grandees, merchants, and those who came from the various districts to be present at the General Dīwān and Administrative Court (*Maḥkamat al-Niẓām*) to be held next morning in the house of Marzūq Bey in the 'Ābdīn quarter. They had a number of rolls written out containing the stipulations and orders which have been referred to previously, sending some copies to the grandees and posting others at crossroads in streets, and at the gates of the mosques. On Saturday morning they once more issued their summons to appear in the old Dīwān in the house of Qāyit Aghā in al-Azbakiyya. And so the Shaykhs of Cairo and those who arrived from the ports and the country also came, as did also the Ujāqs, the notable merchants, the Coptic and Shāmī Christians, and the French Directors of the Dīwān and others, all of them forming a large group. Once they settled down, Malaṭī, the Copt who was appointed Qāḍī, started reading out the decree (*firmān*) with its clauses and discussing it. Then the Director-in-Chief hastened in, bringing forward another roll, and handed it to the interpreter who opened it and read it out. In brief, its contents stated that Egypt was the sole centre (of commerce) and the most fertile of countries and that merchandise was brought to it from distant lands. Indeed the sciences, the arts, and reading and writing which people in the world have knowledge of at present were taken from the forefathers of the ancient Egyptians. Because the land of Egypt possessed these qualities, the various nations aspired to its conquest.

So the Babylonians, the Greeks, the Arabs, and the Turks held it at various times. The nation most destructive in its dealings with Egypt, are the Turks, who in acquiring the fruit cut the roots, and for this reason only a negligible portion remains in the hands of the people. Thus the people came to hide themselves under the veil of poverty as a protection against their evil oppression. Then the French nation, after having established themselves and become celebrated in the practice of war, longed to deliver Egypt from its sad state and to relieve its people from the Ottomans who dominated it in ignorance and stupidity. So they came and gained victory and in spite of this they did not interfere in anyone's affairs nor did they deal cruelly with the population. Indeed, their purpose was to set Egypt's affairs in order and to make the canals which had fallen into oblivion flow with water for then Egypt would have access to two routes, one to the Mediterranean[84] and the other to the Red Sea, with the resulting increase in fertility and income. Moreover. the French proposed to prevent the strong from oppressing the weak and the like, in order to ease the lot of the people and to preserve their good reputation. So it is best that the inhabitants of Egypt avoid disturbances and behave with sincere friendship. Great benefits will result from the arrival of the people who have been summoned from the provinces, because they are experienced and wise. They will be asked about matters of importance, and they will answer. Then the Ṣārī 'Askar will decide what is to be done. And so they went on until the end of what they wrote in their lengthy, distorted style, and twisted, pompous language. They wrote out many copies of this announcement on several sheets of paper and posted them up like the others. Then the interpreter said / 'We want you, O Shaykhs to choose one from among yourselves to be your chief, so that you may obey his orders'. One of those present said 'Shaykh al-Sharqāwī'. The interpreter replied 'Non, non!' meaning 'No, no', 'I shall do something else'. Then he took out some white papers and cut them into pieces and gave one to each one of those present and told them to write their (own) names and that of the person they chose. Everyone thereupon wrote 'So-and-so agrees to So-and-so'. Then he collected the papers and counted them, finding that most of the papers bore the name of al-Sharqāwī. He said 'The majority has the force of the whole', or something to the same effect, 'therefore, Shaykh al-Sharqāwī shall be the chief'. This session went on until sunset, when half the time allotted to it had passed. The gathering got hungry and asked permission to leave, which was granted them, but they were told to come every day.

On the same day fell the incident of al-Ḥājj Muḥammad ibn Qiymuh the Maghribī, the Tripolitan merchant. It happened that there was some rivalry between him and one of the Shāmīs, so the Shāmī Christian incited Dupuy the Qā'im Maqām against him, and also the Ṣārī 'Askar, and filled them both with greed for his money. They sent guards to get him. However, he had premonitions. So he went to Shaykh al-Sharqāwī because the daughter of Sayyid Muṣṭafā al-Damanhūrī was married to him. When the guards found him in the Shaykh's house, they approached him (the Shaykh) and asked him to hand him over to them. After he asked what the reason was and got the answer that it was because of legal proceedings against him, he said 'Tomorrow I shall come and look into his case and study the accusation against him. If he is found guilty, he will be sentenced accordingly and will have to pay for it. The case between them will be settled in the best way'. The messengers returned but the man stayed away out of fear. Hardly an hour had passed when about fifty French soldiers, accompanied by that Christian claimant, entered the house of the Shaykh and demanded that he bring forth the accused. The Shaykh informed them that he had absented himself. They did not accept his excuse and they persisted in their demand, behaving in a most unsuitable way.

Shaykh Muḥammad al-Mahdī and Sayyid Muḥammad al-Dawākhilī set out on horseback to the Ṣārī 'Askar and informed him of what had happened, namely that the man had escaped. He said 'Why did he flee?'. They answered 'Because he was afraid'. Bonaparte replied 'If his offence were not great, he would not have fled; you have hidden him'. He showed great anger and fury. They behaved very politely and sought to propitiate the interpreter, who thereupon spoke with him and calmed his anger. Then the Ṣārī 'Askar asked about his house and store. They informed him about these and Bonaparte then declared 'Somebody will go with you to seal them until he appears tomorrow'. They were reassured and went back at sunset. They sealed his stores in Khān al-Nashshārīn and his house in the quarter of Shams al-Dawla. The Shaykh was informed about this, and he said 'Tomorrow all will be well'. And after the service of worship of nightfall (*al-'Ishā al-akhīra*) a group of soldiers arrived and opened the Khān and the store-rooms examining their contents and recording them in a register. They departed, leaving a group of soldiers at the store-rooms and at the house. When Shaykh al-Sharqāwī awoke in the morning he went to the Ṣārī 'Askar seeking to intercede for him (Muḥammad ibn Qiymuh). The Ṣārī 'Askar replied 'It is impossible to do anything until the man presents himself, since I am looking for him to interrogate him'. While the Shaykh was speaking with the Ṣārī 'Askar, the soldiers made for the house of Muḥammad ibn Qiymuh, where they plundered and took all his furnishings as well as those of the people who were living with him in his house. Next they continued with camels to the store-rooms, emptying them of coffee beans, cloth, and money which belonged to him and to his partners. They even robbed store-rooms other than Muḥammad's. In his possession were many goods deposited in trust for he was much trusted and wealthy (*melī.*)

It was said that the reason for the French turning away from him in this manner and his great fear was due to his being favourably disposed to and in business relationship with a Maghribī living in Cairo and Alexandria called 'Abd Allāh Pasha who was one of the men of Murād Bey and worked in his service. Now this 'Abd Allāh was a human devil who would murder his victim and join his funeral procession afterwards. Once the French had arrived in Alexandria, this same man would dissemble, pretending to be on their side, and he presented himself to Murād Bey when the latter was in al-Raḥmāniyya, meeting him and discussing with him various affairs. Then he returned to the French, and when Murād Bey was defeated 'Abd Allāh accompanied him. Then he returned from the south as if asking for safe-conduct for Murād Bey. In fact he came as a spy fulfilling his tasks, / returning once more accompanied by Rachiteau (?) the Frenchman. Then Rachiteau returned but not he. It was also said that 'Abd Allāh was on good terms with Sayyid Muḥammad Kurayyim, whose story was mentioned previously, and God knows best about the truth of the matter.

On Sunday they went to the Dīwān acting as they had done previously. They wrote the names of individuals on pieces of paper to see who would be elected. Most of the papers had the name of Shaykh Muṣṭafā al-Ṣāwī. So they appointed him as Mubāshir (assistant) to the Shaykh (al-Sharqāwī). Then they exclaimed 'Do you accept Shaykh al-Sharqāwī as head of the Dīwān and Shaykh Muṣṭafā as his assistant?'. They replied 'We accept', and the French official said 'Raise your hands'. So the members raised their hands. Once again they wrote names on papers and these were rolled up. Then they examined the papers, most of which came up with the names of Shaykh al-Fayyūmī and al-Mahdī.

Mosque of Sultan Hassan in Cairo, exterior view (Engraving by Protain)

The interpreter called out 'O Assembly, do you accept these two men to be inspectors (*mufattishīn*) for the two aforementioned Shaykhs?'. They replied 'We accept'. The interpreter ordered 'Raise your hands!' and they did so. To those above mentioned, Sayyid Muḥammad al-Dawākhilī was added. They also set up others like them from the Shurbajīs, Copts, and Shāmīs, thus bringing their number to a total of twenty-eight persons, who were designated as the Special Dīwān (*al-Dīwān al-khāṣṣ*). The rest of the Shaykhs and those who were added to them were termed the General Dīwān (*al-Dīwān al-'āmm*). To every port, district capital (*bandar*), and town they appointed six persons, three of them residing in the town and the other three in Cairo, so that they might be responsible for what went on in the country.[85]

On Monday the Dīwān convened and the town-crier (*al-munādī*) called upon the people, on that same day, in the markets, to come forward to the Dīwān with title-deeds of their real estate and property. The time-limit set was thirty days. Anyone passing this limit would have to pay twice the assigned tax. The time-limit for the country was set at sixty days. Once all the members had assembled, Malaṭī began to read out agenda enumerating matters to be dealt with. Among these, he mentioned matters concerning (procedures of) courts, *sharī'a* cases (*qaḍāyā shar'iyya*), title-deeds to real estate, and inheritances. The members thereupon discussed these matters for a while and recorded these four subjects. Then they asked the Special Dīwān to make their decisions concerning these affairs and to see what were the best means of carrying them out in a manner convenient for themselves and for the subjects. They were also asked to submit their dispositions on Thursday. The days between Monday and Thursday constituted their respite. They thereupon dispersed.

The month of Jumādā al-Ūlā

This month started on the specified Thursday, and the members of the *Dīwān* convened, bringing with them their brief conclusions of what they found to be right. As for the courts and *sharī'a* cases (lawsuits) they concluded that the best course was to leave things according to their former state, and thereupon informed the French of its modes and procedure and the French approved. However, they stated that fees must be fixed so that the Qāḍīs and their deputies (*nuwwāb*) could not exceed them. Thus it was decided that the fee for lawsuits involving sums of ten thousand or less should be thirty per thousand, for cases up to fifty thousands, twenty per thousand, for cases involving one hundred (thousand) fifteen per thousand and for any sum exceeding this, ten per thousand. Thus the Dīwān agreed in ordering the Qāḍīs and their deputies to conform to these regulations.

As for the matter of the title-deeds to real estate, it was a very complicated issue and the most suitable manner of dealing with them was to impose a sum in the most straightforward manner in order to facilitate its collection and prevent discontent. Three categories were designated, an upper, a middle, and a lower one. The amount to be paid was determined according to categories of locality. This decision was then written on a roll which was kept in the Dīwān until the other members had given their opinion about it. Then the meeting of the Dīwān adjourned.

On that day it was proclaimed in the market-places that clothes and household effects should be hung in the sun for a period of fifteen days, and they ordered the Shaykhs of the various districts and quarters and guards (*qulluqāt*) to supervise and inspect this activity. The authorities appointed a woman and two men for each quarter who were to enter the houses to inspect. The woman would go upstairs and upon coming down would inform the two men that they had spread their clothes out in the sun. The household would then give them some money. They would leave only after having given a severe warning to the members of the household, informing them that a group of French would come to inspect in a few days too. All these measures were applied so that the odours of the plague might disappear from the clothes. To this effect they wrote out announcements and posted them on the walls of the market-places as was their custom.

On that day a large crowd of children from the *kuttābs* (elementary Qur'ān schools), blind *faqīhs* / acting as *mu'aḍḍins* (announcers of the hour of prayer), recipients of pensions (*arbāb al-waẓā'if*), as well as those who received legally prescribed alms (*al-mustaḥiqqīn*) such as the insane, the chronically ill, the patients of the Manṣūrī Asylum (*māristān*) and of 'Abd al-Raḥmān Katkhudā's *waqfs* assembled at the house of al-Bakrī, complaining that their pensions (*rātib*) and bread rations had been cut, and that was because the revenues of all the *waqfs* had been suspended and that pension stopped. Indeed, the Christians, Copts and Shāmīs, had taken over the supervision of the *waqfs*, making them a source of profit for themselves.

When this crowd had gathered before the house of al-Bakrī, clamouring and shouting, he received them cordially and promised them that he would attend the Dīwān and speak on their behalf and ease their lot. So they departed to whence they had come.

On that same day boats arrived from Upper Egypt bearing wounded, mutilated, and blinded soldiers. It was said that they had fought once again with Murād Bey and after they had been defeated some were captured. ʻAlī Pasha al-Ṭarābulsī ordered that they were not to be killed. Instead they gouged out their eyes and mutilated them, leaving them in this state as a warning to others and a cause of grief.

And on that day the French put up white flags upon all the hills surrounding Cairo with the result that rumours increased among the people concerning this matter.

On Sunday the Dīwān convened, dealing with matters that they were occupied with previously. Among these they raised the issue of inheritance. Malaṭī called out: 'O Shaykhs! Inform us as to how you divide inheritances'. They thereupon informed him of the injunctions of the *sharīʻa* concerning inheritance. Malaṭī asked 'Where did you get this from?' They replied 'From the Qur'ān'. They then went on to recite to him some of the verses dealing with inheritance. The French said 'With us the son does not inherit, but the daughter does, and we do such and such', and so on according to their way of thinking, since the son is more able to earn a living than the daughter. Mikhā'īl Kaḥīl, the Shāmī who was also a member of the Dīwān, said 'The Muslims decide how our inheritances and those of the Copts are to be divided'. Then the French asked the Shaykhs to write for them the manner in which inheritances are divided and its Qur'ānic proofs. So they complied with their request, and promised its execution. Then they adjourned.

On that day they dismissed Muḥammad Aghā al-Muslimānī, who was Aghā Mustaḥfiẓān (chief of police) and made him Katkhudā Amīr al-Ḥajj (deputy to the Amīr of Pilgrimages). They decided to appoint Muṣṭafā Aghā, *mamlūk* (*tābiʻ*) of ʻAbd al-Raḥmān Aghā the former Aghā Mustaḥfiẓān in the place of Muḥammad Aghā al-Muslimānī and thus it was announced.

On Monday the French convened the Dīwān and the members presented in writing their explanation as to how inheritances were divided as well as injunctions of the *sharīʻa* concerning the division of the shares of inheritance and the Qur'ānic verses concerning this. The French approved of the above and appointed Shaykh al-Mahdī secretary (*kātib*) of the Dīwān and he was called Private Secretary (*kātim al-sirr*); al-

Sharqāwī was appointed Chairman of the Dīwān.

On Saturday, the tenth day of Jumādā al-Ūlā the French convened the Dīwān and presented the list of taxes to be paid on property and real estate. They slightly increased the rates which the Shaykhs of the Dīwān had set. The Shaykhs had set the rates as follows. Six *riyāls* on the upper category, four on the middle, and two on the lower, the minimum being one *riyāl.* Eight *riyāls* on the upper, six on the middle, four for the lower category. What went below that, two *riyāls* and the absolute minimum, one *riyāl.* This system of rates applied to private housing. As for the caravanserai, their rates ranged between thirty *riyāls* and eighteen, the minimum being nine *riyāls.* Similarly rates were set for shops, public baths, and presses and sesame mills (*sayārij*) and the like, each according to its worth. To this effect they wrote notices as they were accustomed and posted them up at crossroads and in the streets. In addition they sent copies to the grandees and appointed engineers and assessors who were to distinguish between the higher and the lower. So they started their recording and calculations. They roamed in some quarters and would come to a place, scrutinize it, and write out the imposed tax. Then they would tell the owner of the place that he must pay half the imposed tax to an officially designated person and the other half six months later. When the people heard (rumours) of this affair and realized that it was true, they raised an uproar, since they found it too great a burden. Those lacking in foresight found it unbearable, but reasonable people said: 'This is all right, this tax is lighter than the former imposition, and easier to bear until "God might accomplish the thing *destined* to be done"',[86] and so they accepted their fate and surrendered / to destiny.

The former group (those lacking in foresight) exchanged whisperings and agreed to follow the way of opposition, rebellion and dissension. Some of the *'ulamā'* (*al-muta'ammimīn*) applied themselves to stirring up rebellion with those people and set out to inflame the masses, summoning them to slaughter the French who had conquered them. Indeed, they preached to them a clear sermon, exclaiming 'O Muslims, the *jihād* (holy war) is incumbent upon you. How can you free men agree to pay the poll tax (*jizya*) to the unbelievers? Have you no pride? Has not the call reached you?'. Thus this deluded one forgot that he was a prisoner in the hands of the French, who occupied the fortress and its walls, the high hills and the low; fortifying them all with forbidding instruments of war; such as cannons on carriages, rifles, carbines, and bombs. The riff-raff gathered, forming discussion circles, and talk and their rancour was stirred up and their hidden fanaticism came to light. They were joined by great crowds of rabble, ruffians, inhabitants of al-'Uṭūf and al-Ḥusayniyya, as well as the Maghribīs of al-Faḥḥāmīn and Kafr al-Zaghārī and al-Ṭammā'īn; inhabitants of lodgings and quarters and the like.

On Sunday morning they joined forces, openly declaring their aims, intending to fight the French and stirring up the flames of war. Thereupon they brought out the weapons which they had concealed and instruments of fighting, clubs, goads, truncheons, sticks, and hammers. He who had none of these, took latch-bars, axes, and hoes. So they set out from all points, attacking the shops and stone benches (*maṣāṭib*), continuing until they filled the market-places and their clamour reached the heavens. They had no leader to guide them or chief to rule them. Sayyid Badr al-Maqdisī[87] came accompanied by those mentioned above and those we forgot to mention, such as the scoundrels of al-Ḥusayniyya and the crooks of the outlying quarters, the inhabitants of the 'Uṭūf quarter as well as others distinguished by their roguery and depravity. Al-Maqdisī preceded them, mounted on a well-equipped horse surrounded by these innumerable groups all yelling and clamouring with a great uproar and tumult their voices ringing out, and replying to one another 'May God give victory to the Muslim', as well as repeating the motto 'May God grant victory to Islam'. In this manner they arrived at the Qāḍī al-'Askar's house where a thousand or more had already arrived. The Qāḍī shut his gates and alerted his gatekeepers. Meanwhile the crowds ran around like wild asses and their fanaticism increased. They threw stones and bricks at the windows of the Qāḍī's house. He tried to escape but failed. So he pleaded with them in a polite manner, promising them the impossible. The people gathered in his courtyard demanding war and an encounter with the enemy. In the same manner, great crowds gathered at al-Masjid al-Ḥusaynī and al-Azhar. When this insurrection was under way, the Qā'im Maqām Dupuy arrived with a great number of horsemen and brave warriors, carrying in their hands unsheathed swords in order to frighten the people by the dreadful sight of them. / Thus he passed through the street of al-Ghūriyya and then turned to al-Ṣanādiqiyya, and to the house of al-Sharqāwī in al-'Ayniyya. The Shaykh refused to see him and pretended not to be in at all. Dupuy therefore went back and made for Bāb al-Zuhūma which was at that time packed with people. He intended to go to the Qāḍī in order to make peace and erase the past. If only it had happened thus the matter might have ended there.

At this point a perfumer (*'aṭṭār*), dressed up in the guise of the *faqīhs* wearing a vest (*mallūṭa*) and waist-wrapper (*izār*), came forward calling out to the people, inciting them and exclaiming 'God is most great, O Muslims. The *'ulamā'* have commanded you to kill the infidels. Make ready, O stalwarts, and strike them everywhere'. He went towards al-Ashrafiyya shouting these slogans to the crowd until they rushed towards Dupuy and beat him, wounded him seriously and killed him, and with him many of the horsemen who accompanied him. The survivors took his body and escaped by the gate of the Māristān (Asylum). The word spread throughout al-Azhar that the Ṣārī 'Askar had been killed. So the enmity became serious and the blood of the enemy was shed. The Muslims could not be silent or at rest and they stood on their guard. They set out from all directions, advancing in small groups occupying the streets surrounding most of the districts of Cairo, such as Bāb al-Futūḥ, Bāb al-Naṣr, and al-Barqiyya, to Bāb Zuwayla, Bāb al-Sha'riyya, and al-Bandaqāniyyīn area and their surroundings. However, they did not go beyond that. They destroyed the stone benches of the stores, using them for barricades with which to fortify themselves and to hinder the enemy's attack at the time of battle. Before each barricade stood a great number of people. However, in the outlying areas and upper regions, such as those outside Bāb al-Kharq, and Zuwayla, the areas of Ṣalība and Rumayla; and those outside Bāb al-Sha'riyya, al-Ṭabbāla, and al-Azbakiyya, in these quarters no one rushed to the support of the rebels, nor made a move in that direction. The same was the case with Old Cairo and Būlāq which did not join in the uprising. However, these rebels believed that all Muslims were in accord. They had forgotten that the cause of all these misfortunes and calamities was but the lack of unity, and the extreme disagreement and dispute among them. Shaykh al-Bakrī warned the residents of the Azbakiyya areas not to revolt and discouraged their uprising completely. Shaykh al-Fayyūmī did the same in the 'Ābdīn and Qūṣūn quarters while the Katkhudā al-Bāshā did the like at Qanāṭir al-Sibā' and Ṭaylūn. Thus they prevented rioting, warning them of the bad consequences. However, what mainly prevented them from disturbance was their proximity to the soldiers' residences, because when the inhabitants of Kawm al-Shaykh Salāma rose against the soldiers who were in their vicinity they met with ignominy. For indeed the soldiers climbed up from behind

The Revolt of Cairo

the houses, scaled the walls, and got inside, killing some people and looting / some houses. Only then did the soldiers give them safe-conduct and leave the people of Kawm al-Shaykh Salāma. However, the rioters held on to their barricades in the alleys. Then a group of French soldiers arrived, appearing from the direction of al-Manākhliyya, and fired upon the barricade of al-Shawwāyīn where the Maghribīs of al-Faḥḥāmīn were situated. The latter fired continuously upon the French, defeating them and driving them away. Moreover, a small group (of French) who had lost their way came from the direction of al-Naḥḥāsīn with the result that they caused them to taste death along with a Shāmī Christian who was among them. When these two episodes took place, they (the rebels) thought them two massacres and their clamourings and tumult intensified, their uproar spread, their lies multiplied, their fabrications increased, and they made statements which were unworthy, forgetting decency and uttering shameless obscenities. As for the Shaykhs, there were those who fled from their homes and sat hidden in their neighbours' houses; others feared their enemies and bolted their gates, sitting with their womenfolk. Others left their homes, setting out for the building of Qāyitbāy in the desert and living there. Shaykh al-Bakrī took both al-Sirsī and al-Mahdī and went to the (chief) clerk in charge of the day-book (*kātib al-ruznāma*) who was a leader and chief among them. They then asked him to send guards to take them to the Ṣārī 'Askar. So he immediately sent some to defend them from attack. Upon entering into the presence of the Ṣārī 'Askar, they found him upset and his mind occupied with what had happened. He asked them what were these evil events that followed one another. They answered him 'These are the deeds of the foolish among the subjects and those who do not consider the consequences of their actions'. The Ṣārī 'Askar asked them 'Where are the Shaykhs of the Dīwān and those who see to the affairs of the people and are entrusted with the management of the government; those whom we have raised, chosen, and distinguished from others?' So they told him that they had a good excuse since their arrival was blocked. However, the Ṣārī 'Askar did not accept this excuse, and said: 'They must be present with the rising of the sun. If they have not arrived by that time and if they oppose us or act stubbornly, we will fire upon them with cannons and bombs, for no excuse shall save them, so you ride now and declare safe-conduct in all streets and places'. So they left him after sunset and wrote a letter about what they had heard. They thereupon sent the letter with a messenger but he was unable to reach

Inside the citadel of Cairo (Drawing by Protain)

his destination and returned without having achieved his mission.[88] Consequently affairs remained as they were until Monday morning. Meanwhile the situation among the gathering crowds became more and more serious and their impudence increased such that bounds were exceeded in every respect. They began to steal, plunder, and loot and then attacked the Jawwāniyya quarter in the district of al-Jamāliyya, completely looting the houses of the Shāmī Christians as well as Muslim houses in the vicinity. They looted property held as deposits and trusts, raped the women and girls, and also plundered the Khān al-Milāyāt (store for women's outer garments), looting all its merchandise and whatever else was to be found. Thus they continued doing such deeds as they desired, thinking that they were free to do whatever they would.[89] In this way their disgraceful acts increased and they did not think about the consequences continuing in this way all the night. Wherever a figure appeared, / they would call to others for help and charge, and at other times they would flee quickly. When they heard a voice they would exclaim 'Come on, O gunners and riflemen', continuing in this way until night had raised its curtain and morning showed its light.

However, the French were alert and prepared by this time, taking up positions on the hills of al-Barqiyya and the Citadel. To these positions they brought all their equipment, such as cannons, cannon-balls, and bombs, setting them up and arranging them, standing alert awaiting the orders of their leader. When the sun rose and the deadline given by the French expired and the arrival of the above-mentioned correspondence was delayed until the afternoon, the rioting of the scoundrels and rogues increased and they began to climb the walls. Meanwhile the people of the 'Uṭūf quarter searched for three cannons which had been forgotten in the house of Qāyid Aghā which was in the neighbourhood of al-Bāsiṭiyya. They then brought the cannons and prepared them for use, setting them up upon the wall and firing them. The French met this action with successive volleys of fire from carbines, rifles, and cannons. At this point the common people jabbered senselessly and behaved heedlessly. They did and said all kinds of unheard-of things. They fabricated all sorts of lies. It happened that someone would start a lie or invent a falsehood in which they would rejoice without any proof of its validity. Then they would applaud it by clapping and making noises with their hands under their armpits. The one who would relate what he had heard would swear to its truthfulness with all kinds of oaths and people would pass the story on at the top of their voices and the women would utter shrill and quavering cries of joy (*zaghratna*) from the windows. Among these lies were that the Muslims had taken the Citadel and that five or seven of the leaders had fortified themselves in it, things in fact non-existent and statements without foundation. Thus they would spread these lies among themselves, asserting their truth and announcing them repeatedly. They also spread the rumour in complete unanimity that the Ṣārī 'Askar had been killed on the Būlāq road. When they heard this their shouting and yelling grew greater and their determination and zeal were buttresed. One of them would exclaim 'The French have perished and died', while another would shout 'They have been killed and have passed away'. A third would exclaim 'The bedouin have arrived with thousands of horsemen'. A fourth would state 'The fallaḥīn have come from the villages and have gathered outside town from all directions and have killed all the French who were at the garbage dump (*kīmān*) so that not even one miserable specimen remained of them', and other such inventions were spread, people swearing to their truth even to the extent of swearing divorce if they were lying.

Then al-Bakrī rode in with the two Shaykhs accompanied by two Frenchmen, and they made their way outside the city calling out for safe-conduct and continuing in this manner until they reached Bāb Zuwayla which they tried to enter. But the mob came upon them in fury and prevented their entrance. So all of them retreated, going to the Mosque of Iskandar and staying there. They thereupon sent to the Shaykhs to come immediately that these affairs might be looked into, and that they might be able to put out the flames of war and extinguish the raging riots. However they dawdled and were afraid to pass through the city. Finally Shaykh al-Sharqāwī rode accompanied by '*ulamā*' (*muta'ammimīn*). They passed through the market of al-Ṣanādiqīn and pulled down the barricades which they encountered and removed the stones / which were piled in the roads. Thus they continued until they reached al-Kharrāṭīn, where they met a large gang of lunatics who fired upon them with rifles and terrified them, leading the Shaykhs to believe that they were French and making them retreat. Then the Shaykhs came back and retreated several times until evening passed. So the sorrow increased. The populace spread the rumour among themselves that the French had sent to them asking for peace, for indeed on the hills they were thirsty and hard pressed. Some of the people were saying to others 'No peace is possible between us and them until they die of misery, to the last man'. Others said 'Out of them all only fifty remain since most of them have been killed by the bedouin and fallaḥīn'. Some of those who feared the consequences and dreaded the increase of disgraceful actions and calamities were advising some of the leaders to rectify these excesses. But the leaders did not pay any attention to these requests and misled and deceived them. Had this advice been given before what had happened until now, it would have been much more suitable and worthy of respect. However, 'when fate comes, caution is of no avail'. The fire continued successively from both sides and the situation became twice as serious. The reply to the letter was delayed and the French got sick of this prolongation. At this point they opened fire with cannons and bombs on the houses and quarters, aiming specially at the Mosque of al-Azhar firing at it with those bombs. They also fired at suspected places bordering the mosque, such as al-Ghūriyya

French soldiers inside the citadel of Cairo, built by Saladin
(Engraving by Protain)

market and al-Faḥḥāmīn. And when the people saw what had happened and the convulsion that had occurred the intoxication left them and sense returned to their heads. They exclaimed 'Good heavens, deliver us from this distress, O Lord Who granteth secret grace, save us from all we fear!'. So they fled from every market-place and crawled into every crevice, descending from the highest places to the lowest cellars. And every human sound ceased and they knew that 'the ultimate remedy was cauterization!'.[90] The firing from the Citadel and dump continued in volleys until the very foundations shook. Some of the cannon balls destroyed the walls of houses and others fell into some of the palaces. Others fell into the courtyards of the houses and caravanserai, exploding with a terrible noise. In some cases foundations were destroyed and people killed because of these bombs. Many women fled to the shrine of al-Ḥusaynī and to the mosque, leaving their houses desolate. So the panic and rumours increased. At this point they wished only for peace and relief. And when the calamities reached their peak and the agony increased and the rebels fled and the fighters went into hiding, only then did the Shaykhs hurry to make an endeavour and to rush to the Ṣārī 'Askar, begging him to put an end to this calamity and to stop the continuous fire of his army, and make them desist just as the Muslims had desisted from fighting, for war is deceit and has varying chances.[91] Shaykh al-Sādāt also rode when the bombs fell and all of them went to the Ṣārī 'Askar and met with him. He rebuked them for their delay and accused them of neglecting their duty. So they apologized to him and he pretended to accept, thereupon ordering that the cannon-fire cease. However, he made amnesty conditional upon the carrying out of punishment against those who had killed, or instigated the riots, or looted. So with these conditions they rode out with a crier preceding them, proclaiming safe-conduct on the roads. And once people heard about this proclamation from one another their souls returned to their bodies and their hearts became peaceful and they came back to life. So they vied with one another in informing each other about the glad tidings. / They emerged from the stables, their appearances altered, and from the warehouses and underground places, covered with dust, continuously castigating themselves and congratulating each other on their safety. So they relaxed and felt safe and that was a little before sunset. Thus the day was spent and night approached and the prevailing opinion was that the matter had not yet ended. Then the Wālī and the Aghā of the Janissaries (*Aghāt al-Inkishāriyya*)[92] passed through the city, in front of them the criers proclaiming safe-conduct for the people. However, the inhabitants of al-Ḥusayniyya quarter and of the outer lanes (al-'Uṭūf al-Barrāniyya) still continued in their rebellion, and kept up the shooting and fighting. But their plans failed because their gunpowder ran out. So the French directed their cannons towards them, constantly firing at them without interruption, until three hours of the night had passed and their ammunition was finished. At this point they were helpless and withdrew. So the French stopped firing at them and left them alone. After the first watch of the night, the French entered the city like a torrent rushing through the alleys and streets without anything to stop them, like demons of the Devil's army. They destroyed any barricades they encountered. They went and came as they pleased and brought the wrath of God upon their heads. A group of them entered Bāb al-Barqiyya and crossed to al-Ghūriyya, rushing about in all directions without taking rest. And they knew for sure that there was no defender or ambush awaiting them, so they had free scope and did whatever they felt like,[93] moving about freely on horse and on foot. Then those wild goats rode into the mosque on horses, entering through the big gate and going out from the other to the place where the donkeys were tied. And the French trod in the Mosque of al-Azhar with their shoes, carrying swords and rifles. Then they scattered in its courtyard and its main praying area (*maqṣūra*) and tied their horses to the *qibla*. They ravaged the students' quarters and ponds (*baḥarāt*), smashing the lamps and chandeliers and breaking up the bookcases of the students, the *mujāwirūn*,[94] and scribes. They plundered whatever they found in the mosque, such as furnishings, vessels, bowls, deposits, and hidden things from closets and cupboards. They treated the books and Qur'ānic volumes as trash, throwing them on the ground, stamping on them with their feet and shoes. Furthermore they soiled the mosque, blowing their spit in it, pissing, and defecating in it. They guzzled wine and smashed the bottles in the central court and other parts. And whoever they happened to meet in the mosque they stripped. They chanced upon someone in one of the *ruwāqs* (students' residences) and slaughtered him. Thus they committed deeds in al-Azhar which are but little of what they are capable of, for they are enemies of the Religion, the malicious victors who gloat in the misfortune of the vanquished, rabid hyenas, mongrels obdurate in their nature. On that night the Lord's host allowed the host of Satan to move freely, because of a pledge which He had taken upon Himself, fulfilling it beyond all requirements. And when the morning of Tuesday unsheathed the sword of dawn and the black raven of darkness flew from its perch, a group of the French formed a line at the gate of the mosque and everyone who saw them when coming to prayer / retreated quickly. Some of the French spread in that area in groups, carrying out patrols as a regular procedure, encompassing the city as a bracelet encompasses the wrist. They robbed some of the houses under the pretence of searching for looted property as well as arms and guns. As a consequence the inhabitants of that district hurried away, seeking safety for themselves. So the sanctity of that place was violated after it had come to be the most exalted of places. And people preferred to live in it and would even place valuable things with its inhabitants which they were afraid to lose. Formerly the French would pass through this area only rarely and venerated it as others did both outwardly and in their hearts. However, after the rebellion the whole nature of things changed, the high becoming low in an illogical way. Then the French roved in the market-places, forming ranks, and in the streets gathered in hundreds and thousands. Whenever anyone passed them they would search him, taking everything in his possession. Sometimes they even killed him. On the other hand the police constantly repeated proclamations of peace and safe-conduct calling upon the people to buy and sell as usual, and to open their shops. The scattered bodies of the French and Muslims were removed and the French had the sites of the barricades cleared up, removing the earth and the piles of stone and placing them aside so that the roads might be clear for traffic. The Shāmī Christians and also a group of Greeks whose houses had been looted in al-Jawwāniyya quarter formed a deputation and went to complain to the leader of the French about the disasters that had befallen them. And they seized the opportunity to take revenge on the Muslims and revealed openly what was hidden in their hearts, afflicting them with all possible blows as if they had shared the vicissitudes of the French. However, the Muslims only attacked the Christians and looted their property because they considered them to be on the side of the French. And then, even the Muslims who were neighbouring those Christians were robbed and plundered by the brigands. The same happened with the inhabitants of the well-known Khān al-Milāyāt which is situated at the gate of the Greek quarter, and in which there were money, deposits, clothes, and goods, belonging to the Muslims. Yet most of them kept silent and did not complain since they were partners in the offence. Even if anyone did complain, no one listened to his claim, or paid any attention to his grievance. The Frenchman Barthélemy was placed in charge of the patrols (*'asas*) and the arrest of anyone who had borne arms or fought or stolen. He distributed his assistants in the various parts of the city to gather information in the alleys and roads and to arrest people according to their own designs or according to decisions of the Shāmī Christians and the like. When they seized some persons and brought them before Barthélemy, they would question them and force them to make confessions. Then he would deal with them according to his own mind and judgement, passing sentence on them as he wished. He would take a large number of them and ride out in his procession with the prisoners bound with ropes in front of him, his assistants dragging them by force as an example. Then he would throw them into prison and demand the stolen goods. Confessions were extracted from them by means of punishments and beatings. They were questioned about weapons and instruments of war. As a result one would point out another who would also be arrested. The Aghā did just as Barthélemy, acting in a tyrannous and oppressive manner. In addition they slaughtered many throwing their bodies into the Nile. During these two days (of revolt) and the following days so many people died that their number cannot be determined. Thus the injustice and obduracy of the unbelievers continued and they achieved their evil intentions toward the Muslims. /

On Wednesday morning the Shaykhs all set out riding together to the Ṣārī 'Askar and met with him. They pleaded with him for pardon and tried to mollify him, seeking complete security from him and an unequivocal amnesty to be proclaimed in both languages in order to ease the hearts of the subjects and make their fear subside. The promise which they received from the Ṣārī 'Askar was mixed with procrastinations. He demanded that they specify and identify the *'ulamā'* (*al-muta'ammimīn*) who were the cause of the incitement of the masses and had instigated them to rebellion. The Shaykhs tried to lead him away from these intentions, but the Ṣārī 'Askar said to them through the interpreter 'We know every single one of them'. For the French had already investigated and identified them and perhaps have found out about some through others. So the session ended and the Shaykhs left without knowing what the end would be. They had also requested that he remove the soldiers from al-Azhar Mosque, with which he complied, ordering the soldiers to be taken away immediately. But the French left seventy soldiers and quartered them in a house situated in the road of the weavers (*qazzāzīn*), setting them up as officers (controllers) and observers of affairs. Then they looked for the *'ulamā'* (*muta'ammimīn*) who were suspected, being Shaykh Sulaymān,[95] the Shaykh of the blind men's guild, Shaykh Aḥmad al-Sharqāwī,[96] Shaykh 'Abd al-Wahhāb al-Shubrāwī,[97] Shaykh Yūsuf al-Muṣayliḥī,[98] Shaykh Ismā'īl al-Barrāwī[99] but Sayyid Badr disappeared and escaped to Shām for sure.

When the French became insistent in their demands, deciding inexorably that those Shaykhs should be brought to them, the Shaykhs spoke with the French asking them what their intentions were and how those accused were to be treated. The interpreter replied that they were to be imprisoned and detained and would be severely reprimanded so that others might learn from this example. The Shaykhs replied 'This would be an ugly deed and most improper, for indeed it is appropriate that the *'ulamā'* be venerated and that they be treated with reverence and honour'. However, the French did not heed them for they had already made up their minds and would not listen to their exhortation since their decision had already been made. In reply to this they cried out 'If their imprisonment is unavoidable then let them be imprisoned with men of their own class'. At this point Satan's gang agreed and detained them somewhere in al-Bakrī's house. Moreover some double-dealer, and I believe him to be one of those accursed Shāmī Christians, informed about Ibrāhīm Efendī, the secretary in charge of the spices (*kātib al-bahār*), that he had gathered a number of those rogues on the day of the riot and given them swords, guns, instruments of war, and cudgels. In addition he told the French that he had hidden several Mamlūks in his house as well as a number of important people. He had provided the fighters stationed at the wall with a well-known cannon-piece which he had brought out from his own house and other accusations without any basis and calumnies out of all proportion. The French thereupon ordered that he be brought in and despatched him to the house of the Aghā where he was imprisoned.

After the riots, when the French had gained the upper hand over the people, they were seized with fear and put on the *cocarde* (*warda*) which they had formerly rejected and disdained, pinning it on their breasts, their shoulders, and their head-gear. Then the Aghā and rulers ordered the people to desist from this, warning them not to make them or wear them. Furthermore, they said 'When you were asked to wear it you haughtily disdained it; however now, after you have openly revealed your enmity and made it public you show affection and loyalty!' So they removed the *cocarde*. They had also hung the coloured *bandieras* upon houses and caravanserai.

On Sunday the eighteenth Shaykh al-Sādāt and the other Shaykhs went to the house of the Ṣārī 'Askar and tried to intercede for the prisoners, these being the five above-mentioned Shaykhs and the secretary in charge of the spices as well as the rest of the common Muslim prisoners who were imprisoned in the Aghā's house, and that of the Qā'im Maqām and the Citadel. The interpreter conveyed their intercession to him and he replied with a hand gesture meaning, be patient. On this they left. When the Shaykh al-Sādāt got up to leave he exclaimed 'No intercession was heeded and no request fulfilled!'

On that day, they proclaimed safe-conduct in the market places calling upon the people not to disturb one another. At the same time arrests continued day and night as did also the sudden raids and looting (by the French) behaving as enemy against enemy. As for all the goods which were looted from Christians and found in al-Jawwāniyya, they were returned in their entirety to their owners. However, of the property stolen from the Muslims none was returned at all.

And on that day 'Umar al-Qulluqjī (the Guard) mediated on behalf of the Maghribīs of al-Faḥḥāmīn quarter and gathered / a great number of them as well as some others and presented them to the Ṣārī 'Askar who picked out the young men and the strong among them. Then he gave them swords and weapons and made them an independent body of soldiers with the above-mentioned 'Umar al-Qulluqjī at their head. Thus they went out of the Ṣārī 'Askar's house with the Shāmī drum (*ṭabl al-Shāmī*) before them according to the custom of the Maghribī soldiers. They went toward the north, since some of the villages had staged a revolt against the French soldiers at the time of the insurrection and fought them. The rebels had also fired at two boats bearing a number of French soldiers and fought them. But when the Maghribīs arrived, they subdued the riot. They razed the village of 'Ashma and killed its head who was called Ibn Sha'īr, plundering his house and furnishings, stealing his goods and livestock. And these all were in great quantities. Then they brought forth his brothers and children and killed them all except one young child whom they appointed *shaykh* (village head) in lieu of his father. Then, the Maghribī soldiers were quartered at Bāb Sa'āda in Cairo where the authorities assigned to them some Frenchmen to come every day and train them in their methods of war and their way of giving commands. The trainees would stand in a row, their guns in their hands and their instructor in front of them. He would give them commands using the disgusting words of their own language. For example, when he said: '*Hardabūsh*!' (*Garde à vous*) they would raise their rifles, holding them in their clasped hands from their lower parts. Then the instructor would exclaim: '*Harsh*!' (*Marche*) and they would lower their arms, and so on.

On that day Barthélemy the European set out for Siryāqūs with a number of soldiers pursuing those who had fled eastward but he was unable to reach them. He collected *tafrīda* (appointed tax) and *kulaf* (impost for the upkeep of the military) from the villages, acting tyrannically in levying and collecting them and after some days returned to Cairo.

On Wednesday Shaykh Muḥammad al-Mahdī, the Secretary of the Dīwān took up the case of Ibrāhīm Efendī the secretary in charge of the spices, subtly bringing the matter to the Ṣārī 'Askar's attention with the help of the Vizier who was known by the name of Ruznāmjī. Consequently the Ṣārī 'Askar transferred Ibrāhīm Efendī from the Aghā's house to his own residence and demanded a statement of what belonged to the Mamlūks from the register of the spices.

On Thursday the word spread that Imperial ships had arrived at the port of Alexandria bearing a Qāḍī 'Askar and such other tales which were without basis.

On that day French boats, about forty in number set out to the north with French soldiers.

On Friday night on the twenty-fourth of the month a camel-rider arrived from Shām with letters, among which were a *firmān* bearing the Imperial cipher (*ṭurra sulṭāniyya*) and a letter from Aḥmad Pasha, another from Bakr Pasha to his Katkhudā Muṣṭafā Bey and a letter from Ibrāhīm Bey directed to the Shaykhs. All these letters were written in Arabic. Their contents after the impressive introductions were Qur'ānic verses, *ḥadith*, and traditions pertaining to *jihād* (holy war), curses upon the French nation and degrading statements about them, mentioning the corruption of their faith, their lies and deceit. The rest of the letters were in the same vein. So Muṣṭafā Bey took these letters and delivered them to the Ṣārī 'Askar who denounced them, saying 'This is a forgery invented by Ibrāhīm the Mamlūk in order to stir up enmity and hatred between us and yourselves. As for Aḥmad Pasha he is merely a meddler and was never a Wālī in Shām or Egypt, for the Wālī of Shām is

Ibrāhīm Pasha. As for the Wālī of Egypt he is 'Abd Allāh ibn al-'Aḍm who is at present Wālī of Shām; for I am best informed in this matter. He is to come to Egypt in a few days in the capacity of Wālī. Then we will live with him just as the Mamlūks lived with the Wālīs'. Enclosed in these letters there was a note announcing the death of Muḥammad Pasha the Grand Vizier and of some other high Ottoman officials who had mixed with the French but the manner in which they died was not known. And it is said that the Grand Vizier was banished to Sāqiz and was killed there. But only God knows the truth of these matters.

During these days the meetings of the Dīwān stopped. The French concentrated on setting up barricades at several parts and constructing buildings on the hills surrounding the city in which they placed cannons and bombs. They also demolished several places in al-Jīza, fortifying the sites extraordinarily well. They did likewise in the old city of Cairo, in the surroundings of Shubrā, and in Inbābā. Several mosques were demolished, among others the mosque near the Dikka bridge and the Mosque of al-Maqs, known nowadays as the Mosque of Awlād ibn 'Anān, which is situated on the Nāṣirī canal near Bāb al-Baḥr. They cut down many trees, including the palms of the gardens, such as those in the fields of al-Ma'diyya opposite Awlād ibn 'Anān and the fields of Miṣbāḥ in the Sākit mosque district. They also demolished the Mosque of Kāzrūnī in al-Rawḍa and cut down the trees of al-Jīza which were at [Jāmi'] Abū Hubayra. They dug a great number of trenches and the like, and (cut down) the palms / of al-Ḥillī, Būlāq, and so on. They demolished the houses and pulled down the palaces. They destroyed the windows and the gates and they burnt all the beams so that destruction proliferated in all these places and the owl hooted in them and the raven croaked.

On Saturday night a group of French soldiers appeared at the house of al-Bakrī at midnight and asked for the imprisoned Shaykhs to be brought to the Ṣārī 'Askar so that he might speak with them. On going out of the house, they found a great number of soldiers waiting for them outside who arrested them. Al-Jawsaqī lagged behind and then raised his voice, calling out 'Hey, this is treachery!' Then one of the soldiers punched him and threw him on the ground on his face. They dragged the Shaykhs along the ground among them towards the Mosque of al-Azbak. Then they stripped them and tied their hands behind their backs and went with them up to the Citadel and put them in jail until the next forenoon. Then they took them out and made them descend through Bāb al-Jabal behind the Citadel where they shot them dead. They thereupon buried them in the ravine at the *Mizrāq* (a place where soldiers train in throwing javelins) at the foot of the Citadel and covered them with earth. However, most of the people did not know what had happened to them for days.

And on the morning of that day some of the Shaykhs rode to the Katkhudā 'l-Pasha thinking that they were still alive. So he rode with them to the Ṣārī 'Askar and the Shaykhs spoke with him about this matter. The Ṣārī 'Askar said to them through the interpreter 'The Ṣārī 'Askar says to you that you should be patient, this is not the right time'. So they got up and left him. The latter also rose and went about his affairs. Then all the other Shaykhs arrived but did not find him so they went back.

On Tuesday several French soldiers came to al-Azhar quarter near the mosque and stood there. People suspected evil from them and stampeded. They shut the shops and vied with one another in fleeing. Their opinions differed concerning these soldiers and all related versions according to their own conjectures, thoughts, and twisted imaginations.

Then one of the Shaykhs went and informed the Ṣārī 'Askar of what was happening so they sent someone ordering them to leave. So they left. The people then returned and opened their shops, while the Wālī, the Aghā, and Barthélemy passed [through the quarter] proclaiming safe-conduct. So the situation calmed down. It was said that one of the French officers had come to visit the guard (*qulluq*) who resided near the shrine of al-Ḥusaynī and sat with him for a while. Those soldiers were his corps and they stood there waiting for him. They may also have done so to frighten the people and intimidate them, fearing that a riot would break out, when the word spread that the Shaykhs had been killed.

On that day they wrote notices and posted them in the market-places proclaiming an amnesty, warning against stirring up riots and stating that the Muslims who had been killed were an equal compensation for the French who had been killed.

And on that day the French started a count of immovable property (*amlāk*), registering it and demanding a stated imposition on it. However, no one opposed this or uttered a single word.

On that day the French removed the gates from the by-streets and small quarters which had no outlet to others. These were the places which had previously been left alone and their inhabitants had been spared since they had settled with the French before the event, by bribing the guards and mediators. The by-streets of the Ḥusayniyya quarter were treated in the same manner. After the event had passed the French changed their minds about leaving those gates in place, and went about removing them and bringing them to where gates were collected in al-Azbakiyya at Raṣīf al-Khashshāb. There they smashed some of these gates and cut their beams to pieces, and transported others of them on carts to where they were setting up barricades in various parts of the city. Others were sold as firewood and the metal parts were also sold.

On Wednesday night a gang fell upon the gate of Ṭaylūn and destroyed it, passing from there to the market itself, smashing the lamps. They broke into three stores and stole the goods of the Maghribī merchants which were in them, killing the guard and then leaving.

On the Thursday the Shaykhs went to the Ṣārī ʻAskar and interceded on behalf of the son of al-Jawsaqī[100] the Shaykh of the blind men's guild who was being detained at the house of al-Bakrī. Their intercession was accepted by the Ṣārī ʻAskar and he was freed.

The month of Jumādā al-Thānī

This month began on Saturday. / On that day the French sent a number of notices throughout the country and posted up some in the market-places and alleys written by the French through the mouth of the Shaykhs, its contents being as follows:

ʻA copy of advice from all the *ʻulamā'* of Islam in Cairo.

We seek refuge in God from all civil strife, be it in open or in secret. Before God we declare that we dissociate ourselves from all those people who spread evil upon the earth. We inform all the inhabitants of Cairo that disturbances have occurred in the city perpetrated by ruffians and evil people who stirred up malice between the subjects and the French soldiers after they had been friends and companions together. As a consequence, a number of Muslims were killed and some houses were looted. However, the kindness of God mysteriously came and the strife was suppressed by virtue of our intercession with General Bonaparte and this calamity ended. For he is a man of perfect wisdom who is compassionate and sympathetic towards the Muslims and filled with love for the poor and the miserable. And were it not for him the soldiers would have burnt the whole city, looted all the property, and killed the entire population of Cairo. Therefore you should not stir up civil discord nor obey the commands of the wicked abettors of disorder nor heed the words of the hypocrites. Follow not the wicked ones and do not be off with those who perish, who are foolish and too incompetent to foresee the consequences; so that you may save your birthplaces and be at rest with regard to your families and religion. For verily God, glory be to Him, "giveth His kingdom to whom He pleaseth"[101] and "ordained what He pleaseth".[102] Thus we inform you that everyone who was involved in stirring up this civil discord, was killed to the last man. And thus God delivered the country and mankind from them. And our advice to you is that you should not throw yourselves into perdition by your own hands but busy yourselves with your own livelihoods, fulfil the obligations of your religion, and pay the taxes (*kharāj*) imposed upon you. For "Religion compels us to give you proper advice".[103] And let it be done with that'.

On this letter were the signatures of al-Bakrī, al-Sharqāwī, al-Amīr, al-Ṣāwī, al-Fayyūmī, al-Mahdī, al-'Arīshī, al-Sirsī, Muṣṭafā al-Damanhūrī, Muḥammad al-Dawākhilī, and Yūsuf al-Shubrakhītī.

On that day the French ordered the remainder of those living by the Birkat al-Azbakiyya and its surroundings to pack and move from their houses so that their (the French) compatriots who were scattered about would come together and live in one single quarter. This was as a result of the fear of the Muslims which had gripped them and to such an extent that no Frenchman would go unarmed. He who had no arms would take a stick or a whip or the like. This happened after they had already felt safe with the Muslims and had ceased to bear arms at all and had played and joked with them. For example, when a Muslim would stroll at night alone and pass a group of Frenchmen they would joke with him and vice versa. However, after this incident (rebellion) occurred both sects felt mutually repelled and each was on his guard toward the other. The Muslims also desisted from going to the markets from sunset to sunrise.

On the fifth of that month the authorities released Ibrāhīm Efendī the secretary of the spices who went to his house.

On the eighth, they executed four Coptic Christians among them two carpenters who, it was said, had got drunk in a wine shop, / and had roamed in their drunkenness breaking into some shops and stealing some things. It was also said that they had done this several times until the Copts finally got angry.

On that day they also wrote a number of notices and sent some copies to the country and posted up others in the quarters and markets, also written through (the mouth of) the Shaykhs. However the text of this notice exceeded the former. It was worded as follows:

'A copy of advice from the '*ulamā*' of Islam in Cairo.

We inform you, O inhabitants of cities and capitals of provinces, you the Faithful. And you, O inhabitants of the countryside, both bedouin and peasants. We inform you that Ibrāhīm Bey and Murād Bey and the rest of the Mamlūk faction sent letters and proclamations to all the provinces of Egypt in order to stir up civil discord among the people and they claimed that these letters were sent by His Majesty the Sultan and by some of his Viziers. But this claim is false and slanderous and the reason was that they were extremely grieved and distressed and that they were most infuriated by the '*ulamā*' of Cairo and its inhabitants since they did not agree to leave Egypt with them or to abandon their families and birthplaces. So they were intent upon causing civil discord and evil between the subjects and the French army in order to ruin the country and bring about the total destruction of its subjects. The cause of all this being the great distress that befell the Mamlūk faction at the loss of their rule and of their being deprived of the kingdom of Egypt. Had they been right in their claim that these letters were sent by the Sultan of Sultans, he would have despatched them openly by appointed Aghās from his court. Therefore we say to you that the French, unlike the rest of the European people, always have had affection for the Muslims, and their creed, and have hated the unbelievers and their nature. Indeed they are dear friends to His Lordship the Sultan, backing him as allies and faithful to his companionship and always ready to help him. The French love his friends and hate his enemies. For this reason there is great animosity between the French and the Muscovites since the latter are inimical to Islam and its followers who profess the Unity of God to the extent that the Muscovites wish to conquer Islāmbūl and in addition plan all manner of subterfuges and perverted intrigues in order to take all the Ottoman Muslim countries. But this will not happen because of the alliance with the French and their love for and backing of the Ottoman Empire. They (the Muscovites) are determined to take over the Aya Ṣofya and all the other mosques and turn them into churches wherein they can practise their corrupt rites and detestable religion of the Muscovites. Meanwhile the French nation is helping His Majesty the Sultan to conquer their

Garden of the Institut d'Egypte

country, with God's will not leaving one of them alive. So we advise you, O provinces of Egypt. / Do not stir up civil discord or evil acts among people, do not oppose the French soldiers in any manner; for if you do, harm, destruction, and misfortune shall befall you. Do not heed the words of the abettors of disorder, "and obey not the bidding of those who commit excess, who act disorderly on the earth and reform not",[104] "and speedily have to repent of what ye have done".[105] What you have to do is but to pay the taxes (*kharāj*) imposed upon you, to all the tax-farmers (*multazims*), that you may dwell in your birthplaces safely and be secure and at rest with regard to your families and property. For indeed His Excellency Bonaparte the grand Ṣārī 'Askar, Commander of the Armies (*Amīr al-Juyūsh*), agreed with us that he will not contest anyone in his practice of Islam, nor will he oppose us with regard to the laws which God has decreed upon us. What is more he will remove all the injustice from among the people and restrict himself only to collecting taxes. He will eliminate the financial injustices which the tyrants have invented. Do not set your hopes on Ibrāhīm or Murād but return to your Lord, the King of the Kingdom and Creator of His slaves. For His Prophet and most honoured Messenger said "Strife is fast asleep, may God curse anyone who would awaken it among the nations".[106] Benedictions and peace upon him. And that is the end'.

Thus the letter terminated bearing the signatures of the aforementioned Shaykhs, written by the secretary of the Dīwān, Shaykh Muḥammad al-Mahdī.

On the thirteenth of the month they killed two people at Bāb Zuwayla, one of them a Jew. However, the reason for their execution was not ascertained.

On that day they removed objects placed in trust belonging to the daughter of Ibrāhīm Bey and her husband from the house of the father-in-law (*nasīb*) of Ibrāhīm Katkhudā Manāw who was formerly Katkhudā Mustaḥfiẓān. These objects were boxes containing gold-work, jewels, gold and silver vessels, household effects and clothing in great quantities.

On the fifteenth a group of French soldiers passed by the Gate of Zuwayla at night and broke into some of the shops belonging to the sugar makers and they robbed them of their sugar and the loss was theirs.

On that day it was pointed out that someone had two cases in trust for Ayyūb Bey the Daftardār so they looked for him and ordered him to present them, which he did after denying several times that they were in his possession. Inside these cases they found jewelled weapons, strings of pearl beads, jewelled daggers, and the like.

On the twentieth they printed a number of notices which they posted up in the market-places, the content being: 'On Friday the twenty-first we intend to fly a vessel (*ballon*) over al-Azbakiyya Pond by means of a device belonging to the French people'. As was their custom, the people made a great fuss about it. When the day came the people and many of the French gathered in the afternoon to see this wondrous event and I was among them. I saw a cloth in the form of a large tent upon an erected pole. The cloth was coloured in white, red, and blue. The pole upon which the cloth was suspended was set upon something like the cylindrical form of a sieve in the midst of which there was a bowl out of which came a wick immersed in certain oils. This bowl hung from intercrossing iron wires running from it to the cylinder. The cylinder itself was bound with pulleys and ropes which were held by people standing on the roofs of near-by houses. About an hour after the '*aṣr* / they lit this wick and its smoke rose into the cloth and filled it. The cloth swelled and became like a ball. The smoke sought to rise to its centre but it did not find any exit, so it drew the apparatus aloft with itself. Meanwhile the people pulled it with ropes until it rose from the ground. They cut the ropes and it soared into the air, moving with the wind. Then it began to sail with the wind for a very little while and then its bowl fell with the wick, the cloth following suit. The French were embarrassed at its fall. Their claim that this apparatus is like a vessel in which people sit and travel to other countries in order to discover news and other falsifications did not appear to be true. On the contrary, it turned out that it is like kites which household servants (*farrāsh*) build for festivals and happy occasions.

That same night at the time of the '*ishā*' (evening prayer) the French gave a display of fireworks, fire-crackers, and rockets in al-Azbakiyya. It seemed that that day and night was one of their festivals because the Ṣārī 'Askar invited the Shaykhs and notables among the merchants and all of them put on new garments. On that night the French passed through the markets very frequently and the dogs barked at them. So they threw poisoned bread to the dogs; the dogs ate it with the result that a great number of them died.

The next day people found the bodies of the dogs in the market-places dead. So the French hired some people to drag the corpses to the dump.

On the twenty-fifth a number of soldiers set out for Murād Bey and also toward Kardāsa because of the bedouin. They also went to Suez and al-Ṣāliḥiyya. They took the camels of the water-carriers together with their waterskins and their donkeys. As a result the water supply dwindled and its price went up so that a skin of water cost ten *niṣf fiḍḍas* if at all obtainable.

On that day they succeeded in uncovering several caches in various places in which there were chests, goods, arms, china and copper vessels in tremendous amounts, and the like. It was said that those who were in Kardāsa were bedouin known as 'Arab al-Ghazw nomads from Banī 'Alī, wandering during the year in the countryside and districts stealing and snatching whatever they came upon. It was also said that they were Maghribīs whom Murād Bey had brought by means of 'Alī Pasha al-Ṭarābulsī, from parts of the Maghrib.

And so this month passed with its major and minor events which are impossible to record because of their great number.

Among these events was that in the Ghayṭ al-Nūbī adjacent to al-Azbakiyya they (the French) constructed some buildings with compartments and places for amusement and licentiousness including all kinds of depravities and unrestricted entertainment, among them drinks and spirits, female singers and European dancers and the like. One of their notables was in charge of it. On the day of its opening he held a banquet to which he invited the notables of the French and some of those of the Muslims and the Shaykhs. That night they set off a display of firecrackers, rockets with firing and illuminations (*shunnuk*). The French appointed attendants, cooks, and cupbearers. At its gate sat a man who would take from every person entering ninety *niṣf* (*fiḍḍas*) and give him in return a piece of paper which would serve as a certificate allowing him to come and go on that day. And when someone would come to this place and occupy himself with food, drink, fornication, and gambling according to his heart's desire he would pay for each of these services according to what it cost. If he took a private compartment which would be his alone he had to pay rent for each month that he held it. He would then receive a key and furnish it as he wished. / This service was not restricted to the French only but was available to anyone who wanted it, whether he be European, Muslim, Copt, Greek, or Jew.

Among these events also was the demolition of the courtyard of the Nilometer (*qā'at al-miqyās*) in al-Rawḍa and the mosque of Abū Hubayra in al-Jīza. The French levelled the hill near al-Laymūn bridge and built towers and artillery points on it. They did the same to the hill which is at the al-Nāṣirī canal adjacent to the Maghribī and they filled in the part of the canal which was adjacent to it with earth. They tore down the Dikka bridge and filled in the area where it had stood with the debris of the adjacent mosque which they had demolished as well as that of houses surrounding it which they had also destroyed. They filled in the part near the bridge, making it level with the pavement at its banks continuing to the bridge. In the same way they demolished the buildings opposite the Ṣārī 'Askar's house and constructed in their place a wide square. They filled in the part of Birkat al-Azbakiyya which was opposite this square so that the bridge became level with the pavement. They also demolished the dwellings opposite this square on the other side and turned the area into a walled-up road running along the filled-in portion of the Nāṣirī canal, adjacent to the Maghribī which connects with Būlāq. They also demolished a great part of the house of 'Alī Katkhudā al-Ṭawīl near his dwelling. And they also filled in the part of the pond which was opposite it and also pulled down the houses opposite. They filled in the mouth of the canal of al-Raṭlī pond and cut down the trees of the garden of the secretary of the spices which is opposite the bridge of al-Raṭlī pond and cut the trees of the bridge, also demolishing its wall which is adjacent to al-Ḥājib bridge and from the other side they demolished the wall of the garden opposite it and cut down its trees and they made it into a road connecting with the mosque of Ẓāhir Baybars in the direction of al-'Ādiliyya. They pulled down the minaret of the mosque turning it into a tower, and flattened its walls as they wished and set upon it cannons and machines of war. And so it came about that the pedestrian who comes from the direction of Qubbat al-Naṣr and al-'Ādiliyya on his way to al-Azbakiyya, passes by way of the above-mentioned al-Ẓāhirī mosque to al-Ḥājib bridge then to the bridge of al-Raṭlī pond on to its filled-in canal until he reaches the road known as al-Shaykh Shu'ayb near the pottery factory. If he wishes to go to al-Azbakiyya he goes to the right towards Bāb al-Ḥadīd. If he wants al-'Adawī quarter and al-Sha'riyya Gate he has to go to the left. And they levelled these roads by evening the high places with the lower. They cut through part of the hill which was an obstacle to the road which is near the canal. They demolished the wall of al-Junayna and cut down some of its trees which are adjacent to Bāb al-

Ḥadīd. They also pulled down the walls and buildings which intervene between Bāb al-Ḥadīd and the public square which is just outside the mosque of al-Maqs which is used as a place for selling millstones. All this in order to connect this road with al-Azbakiyya. They built fortifications, towers, and buildings on Tall al-'Aqārib in al-Nāṣiriyya. They demolished several of the Amīr's houses and they took the rubble and marble to the buildings on the hills and other places. To the administrators of affairs (managers), the astronomers, scholars, and scientists in mathematics, geometry, astronomy, engraving and drawing, and also to the painters, scribes, and writers they assigned al-Nāṣiriyya quarter and all the houses in it, such as the house of Qāsim Bey, the Amīr of the Pilgrimage known as Abū Sayf, and the house of Ḥasan Kāshif Jarkas which he founded and built to perfection, having spent upon it fantastic sums of money amounting to more than a hundred thousand dīnārs. When he had completed plastering and furnishing it, the French came and he fled with the others and left all that it contained, not having enjoyed it for even a whole month. The administrators, astronomers, and some of the physicians lived in this house in which they placed a great number of their books and with a keeper taking care of them and arranging them. And the students among them would gather two hours before noon every day in an open space opposite the shelves of books, sitting on chairs arranged in parallel rows before a wide long board. Whoever wishes to look up something in a book asks for whatever volumes he wants and the librarian brings them to him. Then he thumbs through the pages, looking through the book, and writes. All the while they are quiet and no one disturbs his neighbour. When some Muslims would come to look around they would not prevent them from entering. Indeed they would bring them all kinds of printed books in which there were all sorts of illustrations and *cartes* (*kartāt*) of the countries and regions, animals, birds, plants, histories of the ancients, campaigns of the nations, tales of the prophets including pictures of them, of their miracles and wondrous deeds, the events of their respective peoples and such things which baffle the mind. I have gone to them many times and they have shown me all these various things and among the things I saw there was a large book containing the Biography of the Prophet, upon whom be mercy and peace. In this volume they draw his noble picture according to the extent of their knowledge and judgement about him. He is depicted standing upon his feet looking toward Heaven as if menacing all creation. In his right hand is the sword and in his left the Book and around him are his Companions, may God be pleased with them, also with swords in their hands. In another page there are pictures of the Rightly Guided Caliphs. On another page a picture of the Midnight Journey of Muḥammad and al-Burāq and he, upon whom be mercy and peace, is riding upon al-Burāq from the Rock of Jerusalem. Also there is a picture of Jerusalem and the Holy Places of Mekka and Medīna and of the four Imāms, Founders of the Schools and the other Caliphs and Sultans and an image of Islāmbūl including her Great Mosques like Aya Ṣofya and the Mosque of Sultan Muḥammad. In another picture the manner in which the Prophet's Birthday is celebrated and all the types of people who participate in it (are shown); also (there are) pictures of the Mosque of Sultan Sulaymān and the manner in which the Friday prayers are conducted in it, and the Mosque of Abū Ayyūb al-Anṣārī and the manner in which prayers for the dead are performed in it, and pictures of the countries, the coasts, the seas, the Pyramids, the ancient temples of Upper Egypt including the pictures, figures, and inscriptions which are drawn upon them. Also there are pictures of the species of animals, birds, plants and herbage which are peculiar to each land. The glorious Qur'ān is translated into their language! Also many other Islamic books. I saw in their possession the *Kitāb al-Shifā'* of Qāḍī 'Iyāḍ, which they call *al-Shifā al-Sharīf* and *al-Burda* by Abū Ṣīrī, many verses of which they know by heart and which they translated into French. I saw some of them who know chapters of the Qur'ān by heart. They have a great interest in the sciences, mainly in mathematics and the knowledge of languages, and make great efforts to learn the Arabic language and the colloquial. In this they strive day and night. And they have books especially devoted to all types of languages, their declensions and conjugations as well as their etymologies. They possess extraordinary astronomical instruments of perfect construction and instruments for measuring altitudes / of wondrous, amazing, and precious construction. And they have telescopes for looking at the stars and measuring their scopes, sizes, heights, conjunctions, and oppositions, and the clepsydras and clocks with gradings and minutes and seconds, all of wondrous form and very precious, and the like.

In a similar manner they assigned the house of Ibrāhīm Katkhudā al-Sinnārī and the house of the former Katkhudā Zayn al-Fiqār and neighbouring houses to the studious and knowledgeable ones. They called this *al-Madāris* (the Schools) and provided it with funds and copious allowances and generous provisions of food and drink. They provided them with a place in the house of the above-mentioned Ḥasan Kāshif and built in it neat and well-designed stoves and ovens, and instruments for distilling, vaporizing, and extracting liquids and ointments belonging to medicine and sublimated simple salts, the salts extracted from burnt herbs, and so forth. In this place there are wondrous retorts of copper for distillation, and vessels and long-necked bottles made of glass of various forms and shapes, by means of which acidic liquids and solvents are extracted. All this is carried out with perfect skill and wondrous invention and the like.

On that day the news arrived of the death of Ṣāliḥ Bey, Amīr al-Ḥajj. He had set out for Jerusalem with the Maḥmal of the Pilgrimage, placed it there and then returned to Gaza where he became ill with fever for several days and died.

The month of Rajab

Rajab started on a Sunday. On the third of this month Shaykh al-Sādāt celebrated the birthday of Sayyida Zaynab at the bridges of Sibāʿ. The Ṣārī ʿAskar Bonaparte was invited. He came to the house in which the Shaykh dwelt on the eve of the celebration and that was the house of Ayyūb Jāwīsh. He had supper with his people of distinction and after that returned home, riding.

On that day the French executed one of the soldiers called Muṣṭafā Kāshif, one of the *mamlūks* of Ḥusayn Bey who is known as Shuft. He had escaped together with the other escapers and had come back without permission and had hidden in the house of Shaykh Sulaymān al-Fayyūmī. The Shaykh Sulaymān handed him over to Muṣṭafā the Aghā Mustaḥfiẓān in order that he might obtain safe-conduct for him. When the latter informed the French of his presence they ordered his execution. So they killed him and then cut off his head with which they roved through the town, proclaiming 'This is the punishment of those who re-enter Cairo without the permission of the French'.

On Thursday the fifth of the month the Ṣārī ʿAskar of the Qalyūb district came to Cairo with Sulaymān al-Shawārbī who was the Shaykh of the district. When they arrived they took the Shaykh to the Citadel and imprisoned him there. It was said that the French had stumbled upon a letter of his which he had sent to Siryāqūs at the time of the revolt, inciting people of this area to revolt and ordering them to make ready for the time of the call if he found that the French were losing in Cairo. They punished him because of this letter and imprisoned four of the troopers (*Ajnād*) at the same time too.

On that day they invented a cannon which fired at noontime every day,[107] because among the French the hours of day and night start from noon.

On Wednesday the tenth of the month the criers announced that anyone who wished to purchase a horse or a donkey should present himself on the twelfth of the month in Būlāq and buy from the French whichever ones he wished. To this effect they prepared notices which they posted up in the market-places and alleys. These were printed with the emblem, the sign and cipher (of the French Republic), as was their custom, and its contents were as follows:

'Let it be known to all people of Egypt that on Friday the 12th of Rajab at two o'clock a great number of horses, shall be sold by the French Republic in Būlāq. For this purpose we have granted permission to anyone who wishes to buy horses to do so as he pleases'.

On Monday, the sixteenth of the month Ṣārī 'Askar Bonaparte set out for Suez taking with him Sayyid Aḥmad al-Maḥrūqī and Ibrāhīm Efendi the secretary of the spices in addition to his counsellors (managers — *mudabbirūn*), some engineers, painters, Jirkis al-Jawharī, and Antoun (al-Ṭūn) Abū Ṭāqiya the Copt, and others. He also took a number of soldiers, cavalry and infantry, some cannons, waggons, litters borne by two camels, a number of camels bearing the ammunition, water, and provisions (*qūmānya* — It. *comania*).

On that day they started once again to arrange the Dīwān as formerly but with a new system. They appointed sixty members, Shaykhs of the Theologians, Shaykhs of guilds, Copts, and the French. To this effect they wrote notices, some copies of which were sent to the notables others being posted up in the markets as usual. Those who were appointed to the Dīwān received these notices directed to them personally. / It is appropriate to present the main part of the roll written concerning this matter, in the name and in the words of the Ṣārī 'Askar, because of its falsifications and weak-minded deceit and its audacious presumption in claiming Mahdīhood or Prophethood, and proving these claims by their antithesis. The contents are as follows:

'In the name of God the Merciful the Compassionate.

From Bonaparte the Commander of the French Armies directed to all the inhabitants of Egypt of all ranks:

We hereby inform you that some senseless and empty-headed people who do not foresee the consequences of their actions have recently instigated civil discord and spread evil among the inhabitants of Cairo. As a result God destroyed them for their deeds and malicious intentions. However the Creator, who is Praised and Exalted, commanded me to be compassionate and merciful with His servants. I have acted in accordance with His command and have become merciful and compassionate towards you. Nevertheless, I was seized with anger and intense grief because of the civil discord which was stirred up among you. For this reason, two months ago I abolished the Dīwān which I had set up for you for the good order of the country and the improvement of your condition. And now we intend to reinstitute the Dīwān as it was, for your good behaviour and actions during the above-mentioned period have made us forget the sins of the evil ones and those who stirred up the civil strife which occurred formerly. O *'ulamā'*, Sharīfs, and Imāms, inform your people and your communities that he who is inimical to me and who opposes me does so only because of an error of the mind and corruption of thoughts. Verily he shall find no refuge or deliverance to save him from me in this world, neither shall he escape the hands of God for he opposes the destiny of God who is Praised and Exalted. Indeed the sensible man knows that our acts are His will and divine decree and he who doubts this is stupid and devoid of perception. Also tell your people that since the beginning of time God has decreed the destruction of the enemies of Islam and the breaking of the crosses by my hand. Moreover He decreed from eternity that I shall come from the West to the Land of Egypt for the purpose of destroying those who have acted tyrannically in it and to carry out the tasks which He set upon me. And no sensible man will doubt that all this is by virtue of God's decree and will. Also tell your people that the many verses of the glorious Qur'ān announce the occurrence of events which have occurred and indicate others which are to occur in the future. Indeed the words of God in His book are truth and righteousness which are inevitable in their realization. Once these facts settle in your minds and become firm in your ears then let your nation return to good intentions and loyalty. Indeed there are some of them who refrain from cursing me and showing me enmity out of fear of my weapons and great power and they do not know that God sees the secret thoughts, He 'knoweth the deceitful of eye, and what men's breasts conceal'.[108] And those who bear such secret thoughts oppose the decisions of God and they are

Exploration of the Isthmus of Suez in January 1799

hypocrites, and the curse and affliction of God shall surely befall them for God knoweth the secret things. Know ye also that it is in my power to expose what is in the heart of every one of you, for I know the nature of man and what is concealed in his heart at the very moment that I look upon him even though I do not state or utter what he is hiding. However, a time and a day will come in which you will see for yourselves that whatever I have executed and decreed is indeed a divine decree and irrefutable. For no human effort, no matter how devoted, will prevent me from carrying out God's will which He has decreed and fulfilled by my hand. Happy are they who hasten in unity and ardour to me with good intentions and purity of heart and that is all'.

After this came the rest of the commands and the names of the people who were appointed to carry them out. He then referred to the General and Permanent Dīwāns and the choosing of fourteen members by ballot for the Permanent Dīwān and fourteen for the General Dīwān together with the French directors and managers and other people. He also

(Drawing by Redouté of the Institut d'Egypte)

mentioned the assignment of monthly salaries to the members of the Permanent Dīwān and so on.

On the eighteenth of this month they wandered among the mills and chose from each one a horse or accepted a financial arrangement instead. And that is to say when they had set up the horse market in Būlāq, the millers had bought a great number and every Frenchman who sold his horse made a mark on its ear. Afterwards they would go through the mills and take instead of their own horses whatever (horses) they found suitable or felt like.

On the twenty-fourth Sayyid Aḥmad al-Maḥrūqī and the chief secretary of the spices arrived from Suez, that being because the Ṣārī 'Askar intended to go to the district of Bilbays and they asked his permission to return to Cairo which he granted. So they went back with fifty soldiers whom he had sent to take them to Cairo. Bonaparte went meanwhile to the Sharqiyya. This group brought news (when they arrived in Cairo) that when the inhabitants of Suez heard of the arrival of the soldiers they fled and abandoned Suez, some going to al-Ṭūr and others with the bedouin. The approaching troops looted whatever they found of the belongings of those who had fled, such as coffee beans, household effects, and the like. They destroyed the houses and smashed their wooden parts and water jars. / And when the Ṣārī 'Askar arrived accompanied by the merchants, they informed him of this affair and told him that these doings were improper. So he retrieved some of the booty from the troops and promised to get back the rest or pay the price of the goods when they reached Cairo and that for this purpose they should write a list of the looted property, all empty talk. Indeed when he departed from that place, the soldiers grabbed the property which he had got back in addition to what they had not managed to steal before. Also two boats were found coming to Suez containing a quantity of coffee beans, one of which sank. Then some French got together and boarded small boats and made for the sunken ship in a diving-bell (?) (*ghāṭis*) and extracted it (the cargo) by means of instruments which they had constructed.

During the period of his stay at Suez Bonaparte began to ride about examining the area in all directions of the shore and the land night and day. He took with him as food three roasted chickens wrapped in paper and he had no cook, or valet to make his bed or servant to pitch his tent.

On Saturday several French soldiers arrived from Bilbays with about thirty bedouin bound with ropes. They also took prisoner several of their children, male and female, and entered Cairo with them, conducting them with a procession with drummers preceding them. They also brought three loads of merchandise and some camels which had been stolen from the merchants when they were returning from the Ḥajj.

On Sunday night at the end of the month of Rajab the Ṣārī 'Askar reached Cairo from Bilbays bringing with him some bedouin, together with 'Abd al-Raḥmān Abāẓa the brother of Sulaymān Abāẓa Shaykh of the 'Ayāyda and others as hostages. They attacked Abū Za'bal and al-Munayyir and plundered them. They took the riding beasts and cattle there and brought them to Cairo, their owners, men, women, and children, following them.

On that day they also executed Sulaymān al-Shawārbī, the Shaykh of the bedouin and Shaykh of Qalyūb in addition to three others who were said to be from the bedouin of the Sharqiyya. They brought them down from the Citadel to al-Rumayla through (with the help of) the

Aghā and cut off their heads. Then they carried off the body and head of al-Shawārbī in a chest and his slaves (*atbā'*) took him and went with him to his village, Qalyūb.

This month ended with the general and particular events that occurred, as for example that a number of soldiers climbed and broke into some houses at night, robbing belongings and killing some people in the houses and alleys for nothing. And it happened on the night of the twenty-seventh that a group (of Frenchmen) came upon the house of Shaykh Muḥammad ibn al-Jawharī which is in al-Azbakiyya near Bāb al-Hawā. They broke and removed the window of the reception room which looks down upon the pond, entered by it, and ascended to the top of the house where there were three women servants and a girl servant and the porter. Shaykh Muḥammad, the landlord mentioned above, had moved with his womenfolk to another house and had left some furnishings in this house in addition to these people. He would visit it now and then and sometimes go to the other one. When they got into the upper part of the house those women woke up and screamed. So they struck them and killed them. But the girl hid in a corner. Meanwhile they wrought havoc in the house and took whatever they wanted and descended. Then the porter and his son woke up also and hid. When morning dawned and the word spread the Ṣārī 'Askar was absent. So the Shaykhs of the Dīwān rode to the Qā'im Maqām and spoke to him of this incident. The Qā'im Maqām showed an interest in investigating who had done such a thing.

Other events of the month included the aggressive behaviour of the guards and their severe insistence that the lamps in the roads be lit. When they passed at night and found a lamp which had gone out because of the wind or because of its oil running due to the thickness of the wick and the like, they would nail up the shop or house where this had happened, and would not remove the nails until the owner had made an arrangement and paid whatever they felt like demanding. Sometimes they would deliberately smash the lamp for this purpose. It happened that it rained at night and a number of lamps were extinguished in Mirjūshī market because these lamps are placed in boxes of wicker palm-branches upon which paper was stuck. So the paper got wet and the water reached the wick and put it out. So they nailed up all those places whose lamps went out and when the owners woke up they made an arrangement in order to have the nails removed. This happened in a number of streets with the result that on that day they collected a great quantity of money. They did the same even in the alleys and cul-de-sacs until people had no other occupation but to mind their lamps and to check them, especially during the long nights of the winter.

And judgement belongeth to God alone,[109]
He is the One, the Conquering![110]

Bonaparte in Egypt (Painting based on Raffet)

Notes on the Editing of Ms Mudda

In editing the text of MS *Mudda* I adhered to the principle of presenting the original as the author wrote it without stylistic, grammatical, or calligraphic changes, except in the following instances.

(a) The insertion of the words *nūdiya* and *'askar* where the author had clearly forgotten to write them.

(b) The addition of the letters *alif (ā)* to the word *umarā* and at the end of some verbs in the masculine plural, and of *dāl (d)* to the word Murād where the author had clearly forgotten to write them.

The above-mentioned corrections are indicated by small square brackets [...].

(c) The date at the bottom of the French proclamation in the Arabic language was wrongly copied by the author and is corrected in this edition by reference to the original French document now in the possession of the British Museum (see plate XIII).

(d) The author did not use any punctuation at all and for this reason it has been added in this edition only when felt to be absolutely necessary for the understanding of the text.

(e) In order to give the reader an idea of the original format of the text, the author's additions are indicated as follows:

(1) Additions given between lines in the original text indicated by vertical lines |...| in this edition.

(2) Marginal additions ended by the word صح are indicated by large square brackets [...].

(f) Quotations from the Qur'ān are given fully vowelled, with case endings.

(g) The folios of MS *Mudda* are given in the margin of this Arabic printed edition and its translation. The sign / denotes the beginning of a new folio. Both Arabic and English indexes contain the number of the folio of *Mudda* preceded by the letter f. If the reference is to research on the text, the number of the page is given preceded by the letter p.

In comparing *Mudda* with the other editions and manuscripts of *Maẓ*, and *ʻAj.*, the following abbreviations are used for purposes of identification:

المخطوطة	: MS *Mudda* Leiden.
مك	: MS *Maẓ*. Cam.
عك	: MS *ʻAj*. Cam.
مط	: *Maẓ*. I.
عج	: *ʻAj*. III, Būlāq edition.
المصادر	: denotes the above editions of *ʻAj*. III, *Maẓ*. I and the two MSS *Maẓ*. Cam. and *ʻAj*. Cam.
ص	: page

Within the footnotes the version of *Maẓ*. Cam. is mainly given. Any other version is indicated by round brackets with the name of the source.

Minor differences in the printed editions which do not appear in the manuscripts themselves are not mentioned.

When there is a difference between MS *ʻAj*. Cam. and the Būlāq edition, the former is given because the printed edition is available whereas the manuscript is not.

Two passages in MS *Mudda*, one in the margin (f. 17a) and the other in the text (f. 25b) are crossed out by the author; they are not included in the text given in this book but they are given in the footnotes with their English translation because of their importance.

Notes on the English Translation

This edition of *Tārīkh muddat al-Faransīs bi-Miṣr* aims at providing as precise a translation as possible. However, certain terms, appellations, and titles for which no direct English equivalent was found, are given in Arabic followed by an explanation in round brackets. Those calling for further elaboration, in the opinion of the translator, are more fully explained in the footnotes. For some other terms it was deemed necessary to present the various sources at the disposal of the translator which provide detailed explanations for the further interest of the reader. Words appearing in the text which are European in origin are given in the language from which they are derived or in English if they are acknowledged in English usage. Certain Arabic terms which have become part of the English vocabulary, for example 'Pasha', are given in their English form.

In preparing this translation it was often necessary to compare carefully *Mudda* with *'Ajā'ib* and *Maẓhar* in order to identify or clarify the meaning of various terms as used by al-Jabartī, particularly for the purpose of understanding the many vague and obscure passages in *Mudda*.

The sources referred to in identifying various administrative, religious, and military terms are signified as follows.

(1) Ayalon, D.: 'The historian al-Jabartī and his background', *BSOAS*, xxiii, 2, 1960, 217–49 (hereafter referred to as Ayalon).

(2) Ayalon, D.: 'Studies in al-Jabartī', *Journal of the Economic and Social History of the Orient*, iii, 2–3, 1960, 148–74, 275–325 (hereafter 'Studies').

(3) Ayalon, D.: *Gunpowder and firearms in the Mamluk kingdom: a challenge to a mediaeval society*, London, 1956.

(4) Baer, G.: *Egyptian guilds in modern times*, Jerusalem, 1964.

(5) Baer, G.: *A history of landownership in modern Egypt, 1800–1950*, London, 1962.

(6) Baer, G.: *Studies in the social history of modern Egypt*, Chicago, 1969.

(7) Belliard, A. D. et al.: *Histoire scientifique et militaire de l'expédition française en Égypte*, 10 vols., Paris, 1830–6.

(8) *Description de l'Égypte, ou recueil des observations et des richerches qui ont été faites en Égypte pendant l'expédition de l'armée française*, Paris, 1809–28.

(9) Dozy, R.: *Supplément aux dictionnaires arabes*, 2ème éd., Leide–Paris, 1927, 2 vols. (hereafter Dozy, I, II).

(10) Dozy, R.: *Dictionnaire détaillé des noms des vêtements chez les Arabes*, Amsterdam, 1845.

(11) Gibb, H. A. R and Bowen, H.: *Islamic society and the West*, London, 1960. Vol. I, pt. I–II (hereafter Gibb, I, I, I, II).

(12) Holt, P. M.: *Egypt and the Fertile Crescent, 1516–1922: a political history*, London, 1966 (hereafter Holt).

(13) al-Jabartī, 'Abd al-Raḥmān: *Journal d'Abdurrahman Gabarti, pendant l'occupation française en Égypte, suivi d'un précis de la même campagne, par Mou'allem Nicolas El-Turki, Secrétaire de prince des Druzes: traduits de l'arabe, par Alexandre Cardin, drogman chancelier du consulat général de France en Égypte*, edited by T. X. Bianchi, Paris, 1838 (hereafter Cardin).

(14) al-Jabartī, 'Abd al-Raḥmān: *Merveilles biographiques et historiques, ou chroniques du Cheikh Abd-el-Rahman el-Djabarti, traduites de l'arabe par Chefik Mansour Bey, Abdulaziz Kahil Bey, Gebriel Nicolas Kahil Bey et Iskender Ammoun Effendi*, Cairo, Tom. VI, 1891 (hereafter *Merveilles*).

(15) Lane, E. W.: *Manners and customs of the modern Egyptians*, introduction by M. Saad el-Din, London, Everyman's Library, 1954 (hereafter Lane).

(16) Mayer, L. A.: *Mamluk costume*, Genève, 1952.

(17) Redhouse, J. W.: *A Turkish and English lexicon*, Constantinople, 1921 (hereafter Redhouse).

(18) Salamé, A.: *A narrative of the expedition to Algiers in the year 1816, under the command of … Admiral Lord Viscount Exmouth …*, London, John Murray, 1819.*

* I am grateful to Professor Gabriel Stein for drawing my attention to this interesting book and for supplying me with a xerox copy.

(19) Serjeant, R. B.: *The Portuguese off the South Arabian coast: Ḥaḍramī chronicles*, Oxford, 1963.

(20) Shaw, S. J.: *The financial and administrative organization and development of Ottoman Egypt, 1517–1798*, Princeton, 1962 (hereafter Shaw).

(21) al-Turk, Niqūlā: *Chronique d'Égypte 1798–1804, éditée et traduite par Gaston Wiet*, Cairo, 1950 (hereafter Wiet).

These sources were of great help in this translation. The Cardin and *Merveilles* translations were referred to from time to time but they were of no real value since they offer only a free translation of *'Ajā'ib al-āthār*, glossing over or deleting many important passages and in many instances avoiding precise translations of terms.

LIBERTÉ ÉGALITÉ

RÉPUBLIQUE FRANÇAISE.

LE GÉNÉRAL DE DIVISION

KLEBER,

COMMANDANT LES TROUPES D'ALEXANDRIE ET DE SON ARRONDISSEMENT.

ARTICLE PREMIER.

II.

KLEBER.

A ALEXANDRIE, DE L'IMPRIMERIE ORIENTALE ET FRANÇAISE.

French proclamation by Kléber on the plague

First French proclamation in Egypt

Endnotes

1 The term *munfaṣil* is used by al-Jabartī as a synonym for *ma'zūl* 'deposed' or 'dismissed from office'. In speaking about 'Alī Pasha ibn al-Ḥakīm, al-Jabartī said in '*Aj.*, III, 321: *infaṣala 'an wilāyat Miṣr*, while in '*Aj.*, I, 221, al-Jabartī said: *wa-tawallā 'l-Sulṭān Muṣṭafā ... wa-'azala 'Alī Bāshā ibn al-Ḥakīm.* Cf. also '*Aj.*, III, 211, 230, 317; IV, 164, 196, 201. See the biography of al-Jazzār in '*Aj.*, III, 321–3.

2 See his biography in '*Aj.*, IV, 263–4, 279, and Salamé, lxiii–iv:

3 See his biography in '*Aj.*, III, 167–71.

4 See his biography in ibid., 173. Al-Aghā was his title which he received after having served as *Aghāt Mustaḥfiẓān* (commanding officer of the Janissaries) and his appellation remained with him even after he was promoted to the rank of Amīr and later on Ṣanjaq. See '*Aj.*, III, 173, where al-Jabartī said of him: *al-ma'rūf bi 'l-Aghā*, and that he served once as *Aghāt Mustaḥfiẓān* (ibid., 63). He was the brother of Ibrāhīm Bey al-Ṣaghīr.

5 See his biography in '*Aj.*, III, 64–4. He was known as Ibrāhīm Bey al-Ṣaghīr and al-Wālī was his title which he received after having served as Wālī 'l-Shurṭa (chief of police) (ibid., 173). This appellation remained with him even after he was promoted to the rank of Amīr and later on to Ṣanjaq. He was the brother of Sulaymān Bey al-Aghā.

6 See his biography in '*Aj.*, III, 172.

7 See his biography in ibid., 172–3.

8 See his biography in ibid., 66. The title al-Daftardār (chief financial official or register-keeper) remained with him even after he was promoted to other offices.

9 *Kilārjī*, in Turkish *Kilârci* 'Butler' (see Gibb, I, I, p. 332, n. 4). He was slaughtered by Muḥammad 'Alī during the Mamlūk massacre 1226/1811, see '*Aj.*, IV, 128, 131.

10 The fate of Muṣṭafā Bey is unknown, see '*Aj.*, III, 56. See also ibid., 11, 16, 21, 28-9, 45, 49, 54.

11 See his biography in '*Aj.*, III, 66–7. He was appointed Amīr al-Ḥajj in 1212/1797. Salamé (p. xciv) translated the term 'Emir Hadge' as 'escorter of the caravan of Pilgrimage to the holy sepulchre of Mohammed', and in p. xcviii translated it 'Prince of Pilgrims'.

12 See his biography in '*Aj.*, III, 217–18.

13 See his biography in ibid., 217–18.

14 He was slaughtered by Muḥammad 'Alī in 1811, see '*Aj.*, IV, 131.

15 Known as 'Abd al-Raḥmān al-Ibrāhīmī, see '*Aj.*, III, 171, 218, 252, 285–6, 306.

16 See his biography in ibid., 174.

17 Killed in a battle with the French near al-'Arīsh citadel in 1213/1798, see '*Aj.*,

III, 46. Wiet, p. 52, n. 1, called him 'Kasim bey émir des deux mers'. For a definition of the term *Amīn al-Baḥrayn* see Shaw, 123–5, under *Emīn-i Baḥrayn*.

18 See his biography in *'Aj.*, III, 218.

19 Killed in the massacre of 1811, see *'Aj.*, IV, 131, and Wiet, p. 16, n. 6.

20 See his biography in *'Aj.*, IV, 26–42, and Salamé, pp. lxiv–xi.

21 See his biography in *'Aj.*, III, 218. In Turkish it is *Çoḳadār* جوقه دار 'Valet' (see Gibb, I, I, 352, Redhouse, 738a, Wiet, 297).

22 See his biography in *'Aj.*, IV, 42–3.

23 His death is mentioned very briefly in *'Aj.*, IV, 43.

24 Known as Muḥammad Bey Muḥammad al-Manfūkh al-Murādī. His name is not mentioned by al-Jabartī during the French occupation. Muḥammad 'Alī put him in charge of the customs of Būlāq in 1225/1810 (*Aj.*, IV, 110, where he is last mentioned in *'Aj.*).

25 See his biography in *'Aj.*, III, 172.

26 His name was Murād Kāshif and when he was appointed Ṣanjaq he was given the name Muḥammad Bey al-Mabdūl since the name Murād was detestable to his group, see *'Aj.*, III, 65.

27 See his biography in ibid., 176.

28 Mentioned in MS *'Aj.* Cam. and in the printed editions of *'Ajā'ib al-āthār* as Dhū 'l-Fiqār, see for instance n. 140 of the Arabic text of *Mudda*. His biography is in *'Aj.*, IV, 25–6.

29 In Turkish *Ocaḳ*, active military troops of the Janissaries, cf. Gibb, I, I, 351–5; Shaw, 189; Dozy, I, 43b.

30 In *Mudda*: *fī ṣalāt al-Shāfi'ī*, i.e. during the morning prayer at daybreak (*fajr* or *ṣubḥ*) which takes place at the first faint appearance of light in the east. Among the Muslims of the four sects it is the earliest morning prayer, cf. *Kitāb al-fiqh 'alā 'l-madhāhib al-arba'a, Qism al-'ibādāt*, Cairo, 1347/1928, 158–61. In *'Aj.*, IV, 315, l. 21, al-Jabartī referred to *ṣalāt al-Shāfi'ī* as the earliest time in the morning:

ولا يطلق للفعلة الرواح بل يحبسهم على الدوام الى باكر الصباح ويوقظونهم من آخر الليل بالضرب ويبتدؤن في العمل من وقت صلاة الشافعى الى قبيل الغروب حتى في شدة الحر في رمضان. . . .

In *'Aj.*, III, 331, *ṣalāt al-Ḥanafī* is also referred to as a definite time in the morning when al-Jabartī spoke about *ṣubḥ yawm al-Sabt* 'the dawn of Saturday'; cf. also Lane, 74.

31 cf. Qur'ān XXIX, 41.

32 This is a saying which is mentioned in *Gulistān*, see Sa'dī, *The Gulistan of Shaik Sady, a complete analysis of the entire Persian text*, by R. P. Anderson, Calcutta, 1861, 68–9: وتا ترياق ازعراق آورده شود مار كزيده باشد and is translated as follows: 'And before the antidote can be brought from Irak, he who was bitten by the snake may be dead'. The saying means that the help will arrive too late to remedy the situation.

33 *Ghalyūn*, pl. *ghalāyīn*, *ghalāwīn* also written *qalyūn*: a galleon, a heavily built high-boarded sailing ship with fortified forecastle usually with three decks used for commerce or war. Al-Jabartī distinguishes between a big galleon (*'Aj.*, III, 9; *Mudda*, 2a) and a small one (*'Aj.*, II, 146; *Mudda*, 2a). In *'Aj.*, II, 163, l. 27, al-Jabartī mentions a *ghalyūn* with 21 cannons and others with less than that. Concerning the galleons of Murād Bey, al-Jabartī said that they were with cannons and instruments of war,

see *'Aj.*, III, 168. Cf. Dozy, II, 226a; Serjeant, *The Portuguese off the south Arabian coast*, 134; Wiet, 306; Ḥabīb al-Zayyāt, *'Mu'jam al-marākib wa 'l-sufun fī 'l-Islām'*, *al-Machriq*, XLIII, 3–4, 1949, 354–5.

34 *Dhahabiyya*, pl. *-āt*. A Nile excursion-boat with a big cabin at its poop capable of bearing six travellers. It is also used as a house-boat. Cf. Aḥmad Amīn, *Qāmūs al-'ādāt wa 'l-taqālīd wa 'l-ta'ābīr al-Miṣriyya*, Cairo, 1953, 23b; Dozy, I, 490b; al-Zayyāt, *al-Machriq*, XLIII, 3–4, 1949, 321–64; Shawqī Ḍayf mentioned in his book *al-Adab al-'Arabī 'l-mu'āṣir fī Miṣr*, third ed., Cairo [1961?], 101, that the Egyptian poet Ḥāfiẓ Ibrāhīm (1870?–1932) was born in a *dhahabiyya* on the Nile in Dayrūṭ in Upper Egypt. Al-Jabartī mentioned also a *dhahabiyya* used for freight, see *'Aj.*, III, 280.

35 *Qanja*, pl. *-āt*, *qināj*, *qunj*, *qunaj*: a swift galliot moved both by sails and oars used mainly for freight and sometimes for excursions, see *'Aj.*, III, 59, 119, 163, 244, 280, 281; IV, 199; cf. also G. Baer, *Egyptian guilds in modern times*, 98; Dozy, II, 409b.

36 *Ghurāb*, pl. *-āt*, *aghriba*, *ghirbān*. Grab: a coasting ship of broad beam usually with two masts used for freight and sometimes for excursion, see *'Aj.*, III, 163, 280. Cf. Dozy, II, 204b–205a; Serjeant, *The Portuguese off the south Arabian coast*, 134–5; al-Zayyāt, *al-Machriq*, XLIII, 3–4, 1949, 350.

37 See the French text of this proclamation in, *Pièces diverses et correspondance relatives aux opérations de l'armée d'Orient en Égypte*, Paris. Messidor An IX [1801], 152–4.

38 In Cardin, 20, and *Merveilles*, VI, 25, *plumet*, but according to the description of al-Jabartī the *khashsha* is 'like a big rose'. However, in *Mudda* and *Maz.* Cam. 16b, it appears as *khashsha* as previously mentioned while in *'Aj.* Cam. and *Maẓ.* I, 59, it is given as *khashīsha* and in *'Aj.*, III, 16, it is *ḥashīsha*. The word *khashsha* could not be found in any of the dictionaries referred to. It seems that al-Jabartī's description of the *khashsha* is more suitable to that of the rosette rather than to that of *plumet*.

39 See Redhouse, 1153a.

40 cf. Usāma ibn Munqidh, *Usamah's memoirs entitled Kitāb al-i'tibār, Arabic text edited by Philip K. Hitti*, Princeton, 1930, 135–6, where the author mentioned a similar case.

41 The Arabic term is *'Araqī*. Salamé (p. xii) gave a definition of this drink: '... a kind of very strong spirit, called "*Aráki*" or *aqua vitae*, distilled from *dates* or from *raisins*'.

42 On the illness *waja' al-rukab*, see *'Aj.*, II, 51.

43 Qur'ān XII, 105.

44 Qur'ān III, 173.

45 cf. Qur'ān XL, 16.

46 See his biography in *'Aj.*, IV, 150–65.

47 See his biography in ibid., 284–6.

48 See his biography in ibid., 86–8.

49 More commonly written Ruznāmjī. On his duties see Shaw, 340–1.

50 See his biography in *'Aj.*, IV, 185–97.

51 The term *muta'amminīn* is used by al-Jabartī as a synonym for *'ulamā'*, e.g. MS *Maẓ.* Cam., 15b, *ba'ḍ al-muta'ammimīn wa 'l-mashāyikh*, while the same sentence

became in MS *'Aj.* Cam., 8a, and *'Aj.*, III, 10, *ba'ḍ al-'ulamā' wa 'l-mashāyikh.*

[52] See his biography in *'Aj.*, III, 105–7.

[53] cf. Shaw, 340–1.

[54] See his biography in *'Aj.*, IV, 320–1.

[55] See his biography in ibid., 233–7.

[56] See his biography in *'Aj.*, III, 67.

[57] See his biography in ibid., 289.

[58] In Turkish *Çurbaci*, a member of a cavalry corps of Mamlūk origin; cf. Gibb, I, II, 193; Shaw, 196–7; Wiet, 303.

[59] cf. 'Studies', 292.

[60] cf. Gibb, I, I, 60, n. 3, 201, 284; Shaw, 184; Wiet, 310.

[61] The transcription of the names is according to Cardin, 19.

[62] The transcription of this name is according to Cardin, 19.

[63] cf. 'Studies', 278–83, where he proved that *tābi'* means 'slave' and 'Mamlūk'.

[64] The only dictionary which mentions the term *qallā'iyya* is *Mu'jam matn al-lugha*, by Aḥmad Riḍā, Beirut, 1379/1960, IV, 363a, where it is defined as follows: *ghishā' mansūj yughaṭṭā bihi 'l-sarj* 'a fabric with which the saddle is covered'. It was impossible to find another use of this term in *'Ajā'ib al-āthār*, but in all other cases al-Jabartī uses the word *'abā'*, pl. *'uby* (literally 'cloak'), which is a saddle-cover of cloth or velvet richly embroidered and ornamented, and he emphasizes that this is the Egyptian method of covering the saddle; See *'Aj.*, II, 180, III, 53, 310. Cf. Lane, 143.

[65] In Turkish *Yoldaş* or *Ildaş*, Janissary or fellow-wayfarer, comrade, militiaman; cf. Gibb, I, I, 59, n. 1, 184, 295; Wiet, 313.

[66] According to Holt, 92–3, 'it seems to signify the senior grandee of Cairo'.

[67] See *sanādila* in Dozy, I, 693b, and n. 134 in the Arabic text.

[68] See Cardin, 26. In the note he mentions that the name of the ship was *l'Orient*. In *Merveilles*, VI, 33, the translation is *Demi-Monde*, and in the note the name *Orient* is given with a question-mark.

[69] Land on which its owner has the usufruct rights only; cf. Gibb, I, I, 238 ff., and Baer, 5, 7, 9–11, 17, 38, 40, 52, 154–5, 157.

[70] On *taqsīṭ* see Shaw, 53, and al-Jabartī's description of the old *taqsīṭ* in *'Aj.*, IV, 95.

[71] See his biography in *'Aj.*, III, 62–4.

[72] cf. Qur'ān LXIII, 8.

[73] See Dozy, II, 605a–b; Redhouse, 1944b.

[74] *Tamāthīl* is not mentioned in the dictionaries in this sense, but al-Jabartī describes in *'Aj.*, IV, 198, l. 2, certain arrangements of lamps set in the likeness of various figures such as a ship, two lions facing each other, a tree, or a *maḥmal* on a camel, set in Birkat al-Azbakiyya during the marriage of Ismā'īl Pasha:

ونصبوا بوسط البركة عدة صوارى لاجل الوقدات والقناديل التى تعمل عليها التصاوير من القناديل
فترى على البعد صورة مركب او سبعين متقابلين او شجرة او محمل على جمل او كتابة مثل
ما شاء الله ونحو ذلك . . .

and the term *tamāthīl* may be used here for this kind of lights. Cf. also Lane, 501.

[75] cf. Gibb, I, I, 181, n. 4, 192.

[76] *Aḥmāl* is a shorter form of *aḥmāl qanādīl* which is used by al-Jabartī in *'Aj.*, I,

365: *waqdāt wa-aḥmāl qanādīl wa-shumū'*.... See also the description of *ḥeml ḳandeel (ḥiml qandīl)* in Lane 167.

77 This term is used several times in '*Aj.*, III, 195, *ta'ālīq al-qanādīl*; '*Aj.*, IV, 309, *ta'ālīq najafāt al-ballūr*; see also '*Aj.*, III, 197; Dozy, I, 327.

78 Al-Jabartī mentioned several times cannons on wheels, cf. '*Aj.*, II, 114, l. 21, واحضروا جملة مدافع على عجل and in l. 23 of the same page he says, وكسروا عجل المدافع. Cf. also ibid., 154.

79 See Gibb, I, I, 87–8.

80 See Shaw, 137.

81 See Dozy, I, 290b. A department administers the inheritances of absentee heirs.

82 On al-Jaddāwī see Salamé, p. lxii.

83 Cardin translated *ukar al-fidāwiyya* as '*les boules de fer avec leur chaîne (elles étaient attachées au poignet; on les lançaient à l'ennemi et on les ramenaient à soi)*. On *fidāwī* see Lane, 418; Dozy, II, 246a–b. In 'Alī 'l-Rā'ī's book, *al-Kumīdyā 'l-murtajala fī 'l-masraḥ al-Miṣrī*, [Cairo], 1968, 148, the colloquial text of an Egyptian comedy uses the word *fidāwī* in the expression *rajul fidāwī jabbār* and a synonym in the same sense, i.e. a cavalier or hero, on pp. 146–7 *(rajul fāris jabbār)*.

84 In the MS, al-Baḥr al-Aswad (the Black Sea).

85 In MS *Mudda* the following passage is written in the margin (*takhrīj*) but crossed out by the author: 'Once again they rearranged the Dīwān, making the Special Dīwān a body of fourteen and the General Dīwān forty-six, altogether the Dīwān being composed of sixty members. The members of the Special Dīwān met daily while the members of the General Dīwān convened according to necessity. Secretaries and interpreters were assigned to them. Among the fourteen members assigned to the Special Dīwān were five '*ulamā*' *(muta'ammimīn)* and they were al-Sharqāwī, al-Bakrī, al-Ṣāwī, al-Fayyūmī, and al-Mahdī. Each of these received eighty [*riyāls*] *farānsa* monthly. The remaining nine of these fourteen included Muslim and Christian merchants and Ujāqs. The members of the General Dīwān did not receive a monthly salary. As for the secretaries, they received less than the above-mentioned, some receiving twenty-five [*riyāls*] *farānsa*, others thirty. The above-mentioned Dīwān had in its service a steward *(muqaddam)*, and ten guards *(qawwāsa)* who also received monthly wages. These regulations and appointments were printed on a roll of which several copies were written [*sic*] and distributed and posted in the markets as usual'.

86 See Qur'ān VIII, 42, 44.

87 cf. also'Aj., I, 373-4, III, 304, 308.

88 The literal translation of this proverb is, 'he returned with the pair of shoes of Ḥunayn'. On the origin of this proverb see G. W. Freytag, *Arabum proverbia*, Bonnae ad Rhenum, 1838–43, I, 539, no. 49; al-Maydānī, *Majma' al-amthāl*, Beirut, 1960, I, 414–15.

89 This is an allusion to a verse by Ṭarafa ibn al-'Abd (sixth century A.D.):

يـا لك من قنـبرة بمعمر خـلا لك الجو فبيضي واصفري

ونقري ما شئت ان تنقري قـد رحل الصياد عنك فابشري

See al-Maydānī, *Majma' al-amthāl*, Beirut, 1960, I, 333.

90 Another version of this proverb is آخر الداء الكي , cf. *al-Munjid*, Beirut, 1960, 932.

[91] See ibid., I, 298. The saying *al-Ḥarb sijāl* is attributed to Abū Sufyān. Cf. also Freytag, 384, no. 133. The proverb *al-Ḥarb khad'a*, is a tradition of Muḥammad, see al-Bukhārī, *Kitāb al-Jihād*, *bāb* 157; cf. Freytag, I, 394, no. 28.

[92] See Gibb, I, I, 60–1.

[93] Another allusion to the above-mentioned verse by Ṭarafa ibn al-'Abd, see p. 97, n. 89 above.

[94] Students at al-Azhar living within the mosque or its vicinity. See Lane, 216.

[95] See his biography in *'Aj.*, III, 61–2.

[96] See his biography in ibid., 61.

[97] See his biography in ibid., 61.

[98] See his biography in ibid., 61.

[99] See his biography in ibid., 62.

[100] cf. ibid., 62.

[101] cf. Qur'ān II, 247.

[102] Qur'ān V, 1.

[103] A tradition of Muḥammad, see al-Bukhārī, *Kitāb al-iymān*, *bāb* 42; Dāwūd, *Kitāb al-adab*, *bāb* 59; Muslim, *al-Jāmi' al-ṣaḥīḥ*, Cairo, 1329[/1911], I, 53, l. 19; al-Tirmidhī, *Kitāb al-ṣaḥīḥ*, Cairo, 1292[/1875], I, 350, l. 14. See also al-Maydānī, *Majma'*, I, 377; Freytag, I, 487, no. 51.

[104] Qur'ān XXVI, 151–2.

[105] Qur'ān XLIX, 6.

[106] See Ismā'īl ibn Muḥammad al-Jarrāḥī, *Kashf al-khafā' wa-muzīl al-ilbās 'ammā ishtabah min al-aḥādīth 'alā alsinat al-nās*, Beirut, 1351[/1932], II, 83, no. 1817.

[107] In the text of MS *Mudda* the following passage is crossed out by the author: 'in an ingenious manner. And this is how it worked: they put a mirror of glass at the firing-hole opposite the sun. When the sun approached its zenith and reached its peak on that mirror the powder would ignite by means of the reflection of the rays whereupon the cannon would fire by itself without anyone handling it. And thus one knew it was noon'.

[108] See Qur'ān XL, 19.

[109] cf. Qur'ān XII, 40.

[110] cf. Qur'ān XII, 39; XIII, 16.

Bibliography

(in addition to the works listed on pp. 121-123)

1. Amīn, Aḥmad, *Qāmūs al-ʿādāt wa ʾl-taqālīd wa ʾl-taʿābīr al-Miṣriyya*, Cairo, 1953.
2. ʿAwwād, Kūrkīs, *al-Makhṭūṭāt al-tārīkhiyya fī khizānat kutub al-matḥaf al-ʿIrāqī bi-Baghdād*, Baghdad, 1957.
3. Babinger, F., *Die Geschichtsschreiber der Osmanen und ihre Werke*, Leipzig, 1927.
4. Browne, E. G., *A hand-list of the Muhammadan manuscripts*, Cambridge, 1900.
5. Brockelmann, C., *Geschichte der arabischen Litteratur.... Zweiter Supplementband.* Leiden, 1938.
6. *Catalogue of Arabic and Persian manuscripts in the Oriental Public Library at Bankipor*, xv, Calcutta, Patna, 1929.
7. *Catalogus codicum manuscriptorum orientalium qui in Museo Britannico asservantur. Pars secunda. Suppl.*, London, 1871.
8. *Fihrist-i kutub-i ʿArabī mawjuda-i kutubkhāna-i riyāsat-i Rāmpur*, Rampur, 1928.
9. Al-Jabartī, ʿAbd al-Raḥmān, *ʿAjāʾib al-āthār fī ʾl-tarājim wa ʾl-akhbār*, Būlāq, 1297/[1879–80].
10. Al-Jabartī, ʿAbd al-Raḥmān, *Yawmiyyāt al-Jabartī, Maẓhar al-taqdīs bi-zawāl dawlat al-Faransīs*, ed. by Muḥammad ʿAṭā, Cairo [1958], 2 vols. (*Ikhtarnā Laka*, nos. 59–60).
11. Landberg, C., *Catalogue de manuscrits arabes provenant d'une bibliothèque privée à El-Medîna et appartenant à la maison E. J. Brill*, Leiden, E. J. Brill, 1883.
12. Al-Maydānī, Aḥmad ibn Muḥammad, *Majmaʿ al-amathāl*, Beirut, 1960.
13. *Pièces diverses et correspondance relatives aux opérations de l'armée d'Orient en Égypte*, Paris, Messidor An IX [1801].
14. Rieu, C., *Supplement to the Catalogue of the Arabic manuscripts in the British Museum*, London, 1894.
15. Sarkīs, Y. I., *Muʿjam al-maṭbūʿāt al-ʿArabiyya*, Cairo, 1928.
16. Sayyid, Fuʾād, *Fihris al-makhṭūṭāt al-muṣawwara*, Cairo, 1959.
17. Al-Sharqāwī, Maḥmūd, *Dirāsāt fī tārīkh al-Jabartī, Miṣr fī ʾl-qarn al-thāmin ʿashar*, Cairo, 1955–6.
18. Shaybūb, Khalīl, *ʿAbd al-Raḥmān al-Jabartī*, Cairo, 1948 (*Iqraʾ*, no. 70).
19. Al-Shayyāl, Jamāl al-Dīn, *al-Tārīkh wa ʾl-muʾarrikhūn fī Miṣr fī ʾl-qarn al-tāsiʿ ʿashar*, Cairo, 1958.
20. al-Shayyāl, Jamāl al-Dīn, *A history of Egyptian historiography in the nineteenth century*, Alexandria, 1962.

21. Slane, W. M. de, *Catalogue des manuscrits arabes par le baron de Slane*, Paris, 1883–95.

22. Wright, W., *A grammar of the Arabic language. Third ed., reissued*, Cambridge, 1955.

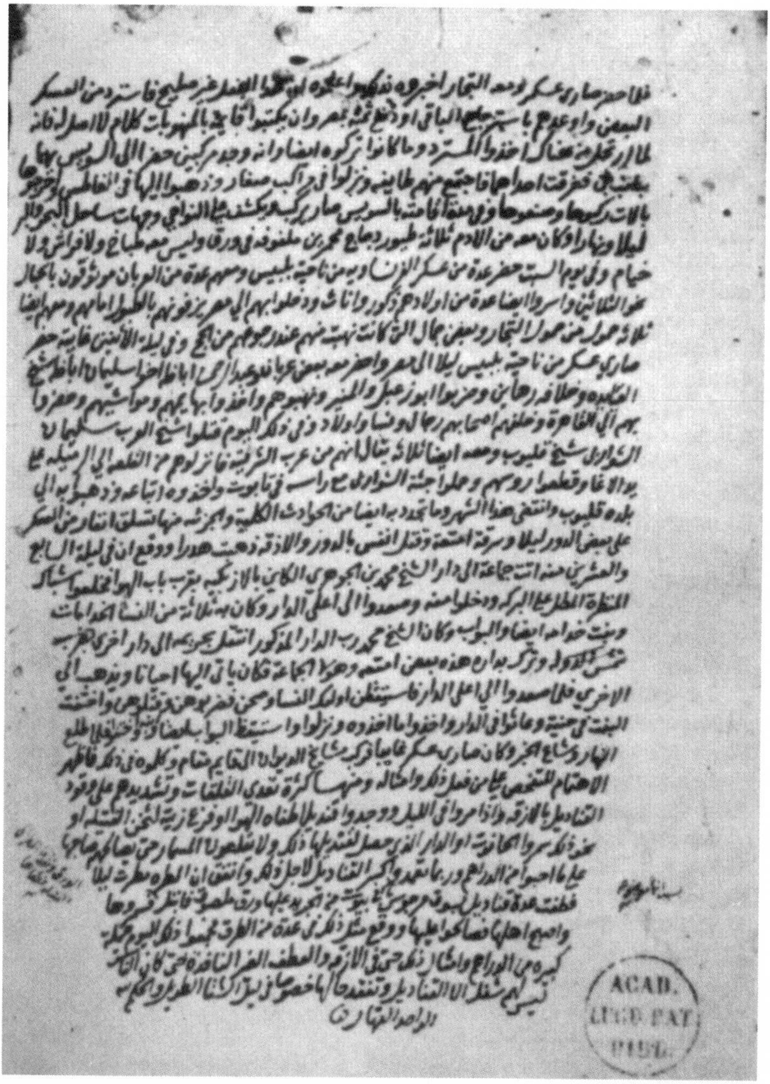

Manuscript *Mudda*

THE FRENCH VIEW OF THE EVENTS IN EGYPT: MEMOIRS BY LOUIS ANTOINE FAUVELET DE BOURRIENNE, PRIVATE SECRETARY TO GENERAL BONAPARTE*

On the morning of the 1st of July the expedition arrived off the coast of Africa, and the column of Septimus Severus pointed out to us the city of Alexandria. Our situation and frame of mind hardly permitted us to reflect that in the distant point we beheld the city of the Ptolemies and Cæsars, with its double port, its pharos, and the gigantic monuments of its ancient grandeur. Our imaginations did not rise to this pitch.

Admiral Brueys had sent on before the frigate Juno to fetch M. Magallon, the French Consul. It was near four o'clock when he arrived, and the sea was very rough. He informed the General-in-Chief that Nelson had been off Alexandria on the 28th,—that he immediately despatched a brig to obtain intelligence from the English agent. On the return of the brig Nelson instantly stood away with his squadron towards the north-east. But for a delay which our convoy from Civita Vecchia occasioned, we should have been on this coast at the same time as Nelson.

It appeared that Nelson supposed us to be already at Alexandria when he arrived there. He had reason to suppose so, seeing that we left Malta on the 19th of June, whilst he did not sail from Messina till the 21st. Not finding us where he expected, and being persuaded we ought to have arrived there had Alexandria been the place of our destination, he sailed for Alexandretta in Syria, whither he imagined we had gone to effect a landing. This error saved the expedition a second time.

Bonaparte, on hearing the details which the French Consul communicated, resolved to disembark immediately. Admiral Brueys represented the difficulties and dangers of a disembarkation: the violence of the surge, the distance from the coast,—a coast, too, lined with reefs of rocks,—the approaching night, and our perfect ignorance of the points suitable for landing. The Admiral, therefore, urged the necessity of waiting till next morning; that is to say, to delay the landing twelve hours. He observed that Nelson could not return from Syria for several days. Bonaparte listened to these representations with impatience and ill-humour. He replied peremptorily, "Admiral, we have no time to lose. Fortune gives me but three days; if I do not profit by them we are lost." He relied much on fortune; this chimerical idea constantly influenced his resolutions.

Bonaparte having the command of the naval as well as the military force, the Admiral was obliged to yield to his wishes.

HEADQUARTERS ON BOARD THE ORIENT,
the 4th Messidor, year VI,

BONAPARTE, MEMBER OF THE NATIONAL INSTITUTE,
GENERAL-IN-CHIEF.

SOLDIERS,—You are about to undertake a conquest the effects of which on civilisation and commerce are incalculable. The blow you are about to give to England will be the best aimed, and the most sensibly felt, she can receive until the time arrive when you can give her her death-blow.

We must make some fatiguing marches; we must fight several battles; we shall succeed in all we undertake. The destinies are with us. The Mameluke Beys, who favour exclusively English commerce, whose extortions oppress our merchants, and who tyrannise over the unfortunate inhabitants of the Nile, a few days after our arrival will no longer exist.

The people amongst whom we are going to live are Mahometans. The first article of their faith is this: "There is no God but God, and Mahomet is His prophet." Do not contradict them. Behave to them as you have behaved to the Jews—to the Italians. Pay respect to their muftis, and their Imaums, as you did to the rabbis and the bishops. Extend to the ceremonies prescribed by the Koran and to the mosques the same toleration which you showed to the synagogues, to the religion of Moses and of Jesus Christ.

The Roman legions protected all religions. You will find here customs different from those of Europe. You must accommodate yourselves to them. The people amongst whom we are to mix differ from us in the treatment of women; but in all countries he who violates is a monster. Pillage enriches only a small number of men; it dishonours us; it destroys our resources; it converts into enemies the people whom it is our interest to have for friends.

The first town we shall come to was built by Alexander. At every step we shall meet with grand recollections, worthy of exciting the emulation of Frenchmen.

BONAPARTE.

I attest these facts, which passed in my presence, and no part of which could escape my observation. It is quite false that it was owing to the appearance of a sail which, it is pretended, was descried, but of which, for my part, I saw nothing, that Bonaparte exclaimed, "Fortune, have you abandoned me? I ask only five days!" No such thing occurred.

It was one o'clock in the morning of the 2d of July when we landed on the soil of Egypt, at Marabou, three leagues to the west of Alexandria. We had to regret the loss of some lives; but we had every reason to expect that our losses would have been greater.

At three o'clock the same morning, the General-in-Chief marched on Alexandria with the divisions of Kléber, Bon, and Menou. The Bedouin Arabs, who kept hovering about our right flank and our rear, picked up the stragglers.

Having arrived within gunshot of Alexandria, we scaled the ramparts, and French valour soon triumphed over all obstacles.

The first blood I saw shed in war was General Kléber's. He was struck in the head by a ball, not in storming the walls, but whilst heading the attack. He came to Pompey's Pillar, where many members of the staff were assembled, and where the General-in-Chief was watching the attack. I then spoke to Kléber for the first time, and from that day our friendship commenced. I had the good fortune to contribute somewhat towards the assistance of which he stood in need, and which, as we were situated, could not be procured very easily.

It has been endeavoured to represent the capture of Alexandria, which surrendered after a few hours, as a brilliant exploit. The General-in-Chief himself wrote that the city had been taken after a few discharges of cannon; the walls, badly fortified, were soon scaled. Alexandria was not delivered up to pillage, as has been asserted, and often repeated. This would have been a most impolitic mode of commencing the conquest of Egypt, which had no strong places requiring to be intimidated by a great example.

Bonaparte, with some others, entered the city by a narrow street which scarcely allowed two persons to walk abreast; I was with him. We were stopped by some musket-shots fired from a low window by a man and a woman. They repeated their fire several times. The guides who preceded their General kept up a heavy fire on the window. The man and woman fell dead, and we passed on in safety, for the place had surrendered.

Bonaparte employed the six days during which he remained in Alexandria in establishing order in the city and province, with that activity and superior talent which I could never sufficiently admire, and in directing the march

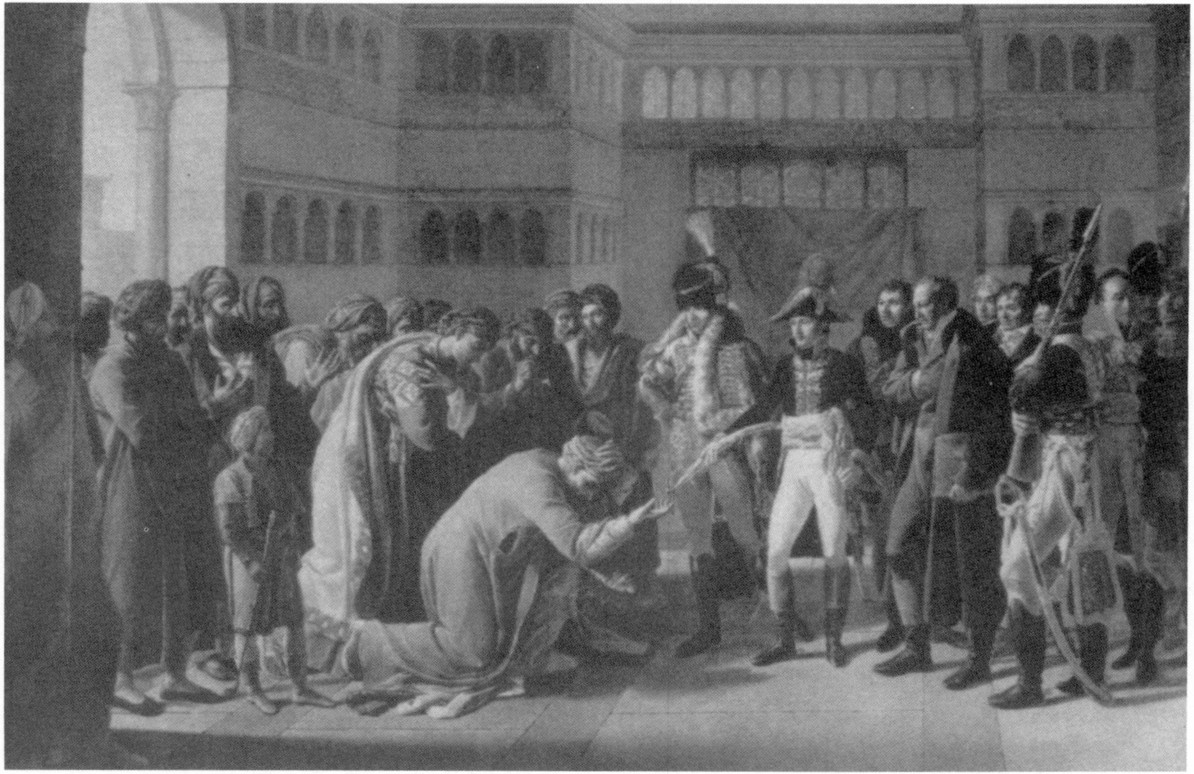

Bonaparte handing a sword of honor to the Pasha of Alexandria (Painting by Mulard)

of the army across the province of Bohahire'h. He sent Desaix with 4,500 infantry and 60 cavalry to Beda, on the road to Damanhour. This general was the first to experience the privations and sufferings which the whole army had soon to endure. His great mind, his attachment to Bonaparte, seemed for a moment about to yield to the obstacles which presented themselves. On the 15th of July he wrote from Bohahire'h as follows: "I beseech you, do not let us stop longer in this position. My men are discouraged and murmur. Make us advance or fall back without delay. The villages consist merely of huts, absolutely without resources."

In these immense plains, scorched by the vertical rays of a burning sun, water, everywhere else so common, becomes an object of contest. The wells and springs, those secret treasures of the desert, are carefully concealed from the travellers; and frequently, after our most oppressive marches, nothing could be found to allay the urgent cravings of thirst but a little brackish water of the most disgusting description.[1]

On the 7th of July Bonaparte left Alexandria for Damanhour. In the vast plains of Bohahire'h the mirage every moment presented to the eye wide sheets of water; while, as we advanced, we found nothing but barren ground full of deep cracks. Villages, which at a distance appear to be surrounded with water, are, on a nearer approach, discovered to be situated on heights, mostly artificial, by which they are raised above the inundations of the Nile. This illusion continually recurs; and it is the more treacherous, inasmuch as it presents to the eye the perfect representation of water, at the time when the want of that article is most felt. This mirage is so considerable in the plain of Pelusium that shortly after sunrise no object is recognisable. The same phenomenon has been observed in other countries. Quintus Curtius says that in the deserts of Sogdiana, a fog rising from the earth obscures the light, and the surrounding country seems like a vast sea. The cause of this singular illusion is now fully explained; and, from the observations of the learned Monge, it appears that the mirage will be found in almost every country situated between the tropics where the local circumstance are similar.

The Arabs harassed the army without intermission. The few wells met with in the desert were either filled up, or the water was rendered unfit for use. The intolerable thirst with which the troops were tormented, even on this first march, was but ill allayed by brackish and unwholesome water. The army crossed the desert with the rapidity of lightning, scarcely tasting a drop of water. The sufferings of the troops were frequently expressed by discouraging murmurs.

On the first night a mistake occurred which might have proved fatal. We were advancing in the dark, under feeble escort, almost sleeping on our horses, when suddenly we were assailed by two successive discharges of musketry. We aroused ourselves and reconnoitred, and to our great satisfaction discovered that the only mischief was a slight wound received by one of our guides. Our assailants were the division of General Desaix, who, forming the advanced guard of the army, mistook us for a party of the enemy, and fired upon us. It was speedily ascertained that the little advanced guard of the headquarters had not heard the "Qui vive?" of Desaix's advanced posts.

On reaching Damanhour, our headquarters were established at the residence of a sheik. The house had been new whitened, and looked well enough outside, but the interior was inconceivably wretched. Every domestic utensil was broken, and the only seats were a few dirty tattered mats. Bonaparte knew that the sheik was rich; and, having somewhat won his confidence, he asked him, through the medium of the interpreter, why, being in easy circumstances, he thus deprived himself of all comfort. "Some years ago," replied the sheik, "I repaired and furnished my house. When this became known at Cairo, a demand was made upon me for money, because it was said my expenses proved me to be rich. I refused to pay the money, and in consequence I was ill-treated, and at length forced to pay it. From that time I have allowed myself only the bare necessaries of life, and I shall buy no furniture for my house." The old man was lame in consequence of the treatment he had suffered. Woe to him who in this country is suspected of having a competency,—a hundred spies are always ready to denounce him. The appearance of poverty is the only security against the rapine of power and the cupidity of barbarism.

A little troop of Arabs on horseback assailed our headquarters. Bonaparte, who was at the window of the sheik's house, indignant at this insolence, turned to one of his aides-de-camp, who happened to be on duty, and said, "Croisier, take a few guides and drive those fellows away!" In an instant Croisier was in the plain with fifteen guides. A little skirmish ensued, and we looked on from the window. In the movement and in the attack of Croisier and his party there was a sort of hesitation which the General-in-Chief could not comprehend. "Forward, I say! Charge!" he exclaimed from the window, as if he could have been heard. Our horsemen seemed to fall back as the Arabs returned to the attack; and after a little contest, maintained with tolerable spirit, the Arabs retired without loss, and without being molested in their retreat. Bonaparte could no longer repress his rage; and when Croisier returned, he experienced such a harsh reception that the poor fellow withdrew deeply mortified and distressed. Bonaparte desired me to follow him and say something to console him; but all was in vain. "I cannot survive this," he said. "I will sacrifice my life on the first occasion that offers itself. I will not live dishonoured." The word *coward* had escaped the General's lips. Poor Croisier died at St. Jean d'Acre.

On the 10th of July our headquarters were established at Rahmahanie'h, where they remained during the 11th and 12th. At this place commences the canal which was cut by Alexander to convey water to his new city, and to facilitate commercial intercourse between Europe and the East.

The flotilla, commanded by the brave chief of division Perrée, had just arrived from Rosetta. Perrée was on board the xebec Cerf.[2] Bonaparte placed on board the Cerf and the other vessels of the flotilla those individuals who, not being military, could not be serviceable in engagements, and whose horses served to mount a few of the troops.

On the night of the 14th of July the General-in-Chief directed his march towards the south, along the left bank of the Nile. The flotilla sailed up the river parallel with the left wing of the army. But the force of the wind, which at this season blows regularly from the Mediterranean into the valley of the Nile, carried the flotilla far in advance of the army, and frustrated the plan of their mutually defending and supporting each other. The flotilla thus unprotected fell in with seven Turkish gunboats coming from Cairo, and was exposed simultaneously to their fire and to that of the Mamelukes, fellahs, and Arabs who lined both banks of the river. They had small guns mounted on camels.

Perrée cast anchor, and an engagement commenced at nine o'clock on the 14th of July, and continued till half-past twelve.

At the same time the General-in-Chief met and attacked a corps of about 4,000 Mamelukes. His object, as he afterwards said, was to turn the corps by the left of the village of Chebreisse, and to drive it upon the Nile.

About eleven in the morning Perrée told me that the Turks were doing us more harm than we were doing them; that our ammunition would soon be exhausted; that the army was far inland, and that if it did not make a move to the left there would be no hope for us. Several vessels had already been boarded and taken by the Turks, who massacred the crews before our eyes, and with barbarous ferocity showed us the heads of the slaughtered men.

Perrée, at considerable risk, despatched several persons to inform the General-in-Chief of the desperate situation of the flotilla. The cannonade which Bonaparte had heard since the morning, and the explosion of a Turkish gunboat, which was blown up by the artillery of the xebec, led him to fear that our situation was really perilous. He therefore made a movement to the left, in the direction of the Nile and Chebreisse, beat the Mamelukes, and forced them to retire on Cairo. At sight of the French troops the commander of the Turkish flotilla weighed anchor and sailed up the Nile. The two banks of the river were evacuated, and the flotilla escaped the destruction which a short time before had appeared inevitable. Some writers have alleged that the Turkish flotilla was destroyed in this engagement. The truth is, the Turks did us considerable injury, while on their part they suffered but little. We had twenty men killed and several wounded. Upwards of 1,500 cannon-shots were fired during the action.

General Berthier, in his narrative of the Egyptian expedition, enumerates the individuals who, though not in the military service, assisted Perrée in this unequal and dangerous engagement. He mentions Monge, Berthollet, Andréossy, the paymaster, Junot, and Bourrienne, secretary to the General-in-Chief. It has also been stated that Sucy, the commissary-general, was seriously wounded while bravely defending a gunboat laden with provisions; but this is incorrect.

We had no communication with the army until the 23d of July. On the 22d we came in sight of the Pyramids, and were informed that we were only about ten leagues from Gizeh, where they are situated. The cannonade which we heard, and which augmented in proportion as the north wind diminished, announced a serious engagement; and that same day we saw the banks of the Nile strewed with heaps of bodies, which the waves were every moment washing into the sea. This horrible spectacle, the silence of the surrounding villages, which had hitherto been armed against us, and the cessation of the firing from the banks of the river, led us to infer, with the tolerable certainty, that a battle fatal to the Mamelukes had been fought. The misery we suffered on our passage from Rahmahanie'h to Gizeh is indescribable. We lived for eleven days on melons and water, besides being momentarily exposed to the musketry of the Arabs and the fellahs. We luckily escaped with but a few killed and wounded. The rising of the Nile was only beginning. The shallowness of the river near Cairo obliged us to leave the xebec and get on board a djerm. We reached Gizeh at three in the afternoon of the 23d of July.

When I saluted the General, whom I had not seen for twelve days, he thus addressed me: "So you are here, are you? Do you know that you have all of you been the cause of my not following up the battle of Chebreisse? I was to save you, Monge, Berthollet, and the others on board the flotilla that

Battle of the Pyramids (Painting by Lejeune)

I hurried the movement of my left upon the Nile before my right had turned Chebreisse. But for that, not a single Mameluke would have escaped."

"I thank you for my own part," replied I; "but in conscience could you have abandoned us, after taking away our horses, and making us go on board the xebec, whether we would or not?" He laughed, and then told me how sorry he was for the wound of Sucy, and the death of many useful men, whose places could not possibly be filled up.

He made me write a letter to his brother Louis, informing him that he had gained a complete victory over the Mamelukes at Embabeh, opposite Boulac, and that the enemy's loss was 2,000 men killed and wounded, 40 guns, and a great number of horses.

The occupation of Cairo was the immediate consequence of the victory of Embabeh. Bonaparte established his headquarters in the house of Elfy Bey, in the great square of Ezbekye'h.

The march of the French army to Cairo was attended by an uninterrupted succession of combats and victories. We had won the battles of Rahmahanie'h, Chebreisse, and the Pyramids. The Mamelukes were defeated, and their chief, Mourad Bey, was obliged to fly into Upper Egypt. Bonaparte found no obstacle to oppose his entrance into the capital of Egypt, after a campaign of only twenty days.

No conquerer, perhaps, ever enjoyed a victory so much as Bonaparte, and yet no one was ever less inclined to abuse his triumphs.

We entered Cairo on the 24th of July, and the General-in-Chief immediately directed his attention to the civil and military organisation of the country. Only those who saw him in the vigour of his youth can form an idea of his extraordinary intelligence and activity. Nothing escaped his observation. Egypt had long been the object of his study; and in a few weeks he was as well acquainted with the country as if he had lived in it ten years. He issued orders for observing the strictest discipline, and these orders were punctually obeyed.

The mosques, the civil and religious institutions, the harems, the women, the customs of the country,—all were scrupulously respected. A few days after they entered Cairo, the French were freely admitted into the shops, and were seen sociably smoking their pipes with the inhabitants, assisting them in their occupations, and playing with their children.

The day after his arrival in Cairo, Bonaparte addressed to his brother Joseph the following letter, which was intercepted and printed. Its authenticity has been doubted, but I saw Napoleon write it, and he read it to me before he sent it off.

CAIRO
7th Thermidor (25th July, 1798).

You will see in the public papers the bulletins of the battles and conquest of Egypt, which were sufficiently contested to add another wreath to the laurels of this army. Egypt is richer than any country in the world in corn, rice, vegetables, and cattle. But the people are in a state of utter barbarism. We cannot procure money, even to pay the troops. I may be in France in two months.

Engage a country-house, to be ready for me on my arrival, either near Paris or in Burgundy, where I mean to pass the winter.[3]

BONAPARTE.

This announcement of his departure to his brother is corroborated by a note which he despatched some days after, enumerating the supplies and individuals which he wished to have sent to Egypt. His note proves, more convincingly than any arguments, that Bonaparte earnestly wished to preserve his conquest, and to make it a French colony. It must be borne in mind that the note here alluded to, as well as the letter above quoted, was written long before the destruction of the fleet.

From the details I have already given respecting Bonaparte's plans for colonising Egypt, it will be seen that his energy of mind urged him to adopt anticipatory measures for the accomplishment of objects which were never realised. During the short intervals in which he sheathed his sword he planned provisional governments for the towns and provinces occupied by the French troops, and he adroitly contrived to serve the interests of his army without appearing to violate those of the country. After he had been four days at Cairo, during which time he employed himself in examining everything, and consulting every individual from whom he could obtain useful information, he published the following order,—

HEADQUARTERS, CAIRO,
9th Thermidor, year VI.

BONAPARTE, MEMBER OF THE NATIONAL INSTITUTE, AND GENERAL-IN-CHIEF, ORDERS,—

Art. 1. There shall be in each province of Egypt a divan, composed of seven individuals, whose duty will be to superintend the interests of the province; to communicate to me any complaints that may be made; to prevent warfare among the different villages; to apprehend and punish criminals (for which purpose they may demand assistance from the French commandant); and to take every opportunity of enlightening the people.

Art. 2. There shall be in each province an aga of the Janizaries, maintaining constant communication with the French commandant. He shall have with him a company of sixty armed natives, whom he may take wherever he pleases, for the maintenance of good order, subordination, and tranquility.

Art. 3. There shall be in each province an intendant, whose business will be to levy the miri, the feddam, and the other contributions which formerly belonged to the Mamelukes, but which now belong to the French Republic. The intendants shall have as many agents as may be necessary.

Art. 4. The said intendant shall have a French agent to correspond with the Finance Department, and to execute all the orders he may receive.

BONAPARTE.

While Bonaparte was thus actively taking measures for the organisation of the country,[4] General Desaix had marched into Upper Egypt in pursuit of Mourad Bey. We learned that Ibrahim, who, next to Mourad, was the most influential of the beys, had proceeded towards Syria, by the way of Belbeis and Salehye'h. The General-in-Chief immediately determined to march in person against that formidable enemy, and he left Cairo about fifteen days after he had entered it. It is unnecessary to describe the well-known engagement in which Bonaparte drove Ibrahim back upon El-Arish; besides, I do not enter minutely into the details of battles, my chief object being to record events which I personally witnessed.

At the battle of Salehye'h, Bonaparte thought he had lost one of his aides-de-camp, Sulkowsky, to whom he was much attached, and who had been with us during the whole of the campaign of Italy. On the field of battle one object of regret cannot long engross the mind; yet, on his return to Cairo, Bonaparte frequently spoke to me of Sulkowsky in terms of unfeigned sorrow.

"I cannot," said he, one day, "sufficiently admire the noble spirit and determined courage of poor Sulkowsky." He often said that Sulkowsky would have been a valuable aid to whoever might undertake the resuscitation of Poland. Fortunately that brave officer was not killed on that occasion, though seriously wounded. He was, however, killed shortly after.

The destruction of the French squadron in the roads of Aboukir occurred during the absence of the General-in-Chief. This event happened on the 1st of August. The details are generally known; but there is one circumstance to which I cannot refrain from alluding, and which excited deep interest at the time. This was the heroic courage of the son of Casabianca, the captain of the Orient. Casabianca was among the wounded, and when the vessel was blown up, his son, a lad of ten years of age, preferred perishing with him rather than saving himself, when one of the seamen had secured him the means of escape. I told the aide-de-camp, sent by General Kléber, who had the command of Alexandria, that the General-in-Chief was near Salehye'h. He proceeded thither immediately, and Bonaparte hastened back to Cairo, a distance of about thirty-three leagues.

In spite of any assertions that may have been made to the contrary, the fact is, that as soon as the French troops set foot in Egypt, they were filled with dissatisfaction, and ardently longed to return home.[5] The illusion of the expedition had disappeared, and only its reality remained. What bitter murmuring have I not heard from Murat, Lannes, Berthier, Bessières, and others! Their complaints were, indeed, often so unmeasured as almost to amount to sedition. This greatly vexed Bonaparte, and drew from him severe reproaches and violent language.[6] When the news arrived of the loss of the fleet, discontent increased. All who had acquired fortunes under Napoleon now began to fear that they would never enjoy them. All turned their thoughts to Paris, and its amusements, and were utterly disheartened at the idea of being separated from their homes and their friends for a period, the termination of which it was impossible to foresee.

The catastrophe of Aboukir came like a thunderbolt upon the General-in-Chief. In spite of all his energy and fortitude, he was deeply distressed by the disasters which now assailed him. To the painful feelings excited by the complaints and dejection of his companies in arms was now added the irreparable misfortune of the burning of our fleet. He measured the fatal consequences of this event at a single glance. We were now cut off from all communication with France, and all hope of returning thither, except by a degrading capitulation with an implacable and hated enemy. Bonaparte had lost all chance of preserving his conquest, and to him this was indeed a

Battle of Aboukir

bitter reflection. And at what a time did this disaster befall him? At the very moment when he was about to apply for the aid of the mother-country.

From what General Bonaparte communicated to me previously to the 1st of August, his object was, having once secured the possession of Egypt, to return to Toulon with the fleet; then to send troops and provisions of every kind to Egypt; and next to combine with the fleet all the forces that could be supplied, not only by France, but by her allies, for the purpose of attacking England. It is certain that previously to his departure for Egypt he had laid before the Directory a note relative to his plans. He always regarded a descent upon England as possible, though in its result fatal, so long as we should be inferior in naval strength; but he hoped by various manœuvres to secure a superiority on one point.

His intention was to return to France. Availing himself of the departure of the English fleet for the Mediterranean, the alarm excited by his Egyptian expedition, the panic that would be inspired by his sudden appearance at Boulogne, and his preparations against England, he hoped to oblige that power to withdraw her naval force from the Mediterranean, and to prevent her sending out troops to Egypt. This project was often in his head. He would have thought it sublime to date an order of the day from the ruins of Memphis, and three months later, one from London. The loss of the fleet converted all these bold conceptions into mere romantic visions.

When alone with me he gave free vent to his emotion. I observed to him that the disaster was doubtless great, but that it would have been infinitely more irreparable had Nelson fallen in with us at Malta, or had he waited for us four-and-twenty hours before Alexandria, or in the open sea. "Any one of these events," said I, "which were not only possible, but probable, would have deprived us of every resource. We are blockaded here, but we have provisions and money. Let us then wait patiently to see what the Directory will do for us."—"The Directory!" exclaimed he, angrily, "the Directory is composed of a set of scoundrels! they envy and hate me, and would gladly let me perish here. Besides, you see how dissatisfied the whole army is: not a man is willing to stay."

The pleasing illusions which were cherished at the outset of the expedition vanished long before our arrival in Cairo. Egypt was no longer the empire of the Ptolemies, covered with populous and wealthy cities; it now presented one unvaried scene of devastation and misery. Instead of being aided by the inhabitants, whom we had ruined, for the sake of delivering them from the yoke of the beys, we found all against us: Mamelukes, Arabs, and fellahs. No Frenchman was secure of his life who happened to stray half a mile from any inhabited place, or the corps to which he belonged. The hostility which prevailed against us and the discontent of the army were clearly developed in the numerous letters which were written to France at the time, and intercepted.

The gloomy reflections which at first assailed Bonaparte were speedily banished; and he soon recovered the fortitude and presence of mind which had been for a moment shaken by the overwhelming news from Aboukir. He, however, sometimes repeated, in a tone which it would be difficult to describe, "Unfortunate Brueys, what have you done!"

I have remarked that in some chance observations which escaped Napoleon at St. Helena he endeavoured to throw all the blame of the affair on Admiral Brueys. Persons who are determined to make Bonaparte an exception to human nature have unjustly reproached the Admiral for the loss of the fleet.

The loss of the fleet convinced General Bonaparte of the necessity of speedily and effectively organising Egypt, where everything denoted that we should stay for a considerable time, except in the event of a forced evacuation, which the General was far from foreseeing or fearing. The distance of Ibrahim Bey and Mourad Bey now left him a little at rest. War, fortifications, taxation, government, the organisation of the divans, trade, art, and science, all occupied his attention. Orders and instructions were immediately despatched, if not to repair the defeat, at least to avert the first danger that might ensue from it. On the 21st of August, Bonaparte established at Cairo an institute of the arts and sciences, of which he subsequently appointed me a member in the room of M. de Sucy, who was obliged to return to France, in consequence of the wound he received on board the flotilla in the Nile.[7]

In founding this Institute, Bonaparte wished to afford an example of his ideas of civilisation. The minutes of the sittings of that learned body, which have been printed, bear evidence of its utility, and of Napoleon's extended views. The objects of the Institute were the advancement and propagation of information in Egypt, and the study and publication of all facts relating to the natural history, trade, and antiquities of the ancient country.

On the 18th, Bonaparte was present at the ceremony of opening the dike of the canal of Cairo, which receives the water of the Nile when it reaches the height fixed by the Mequyas.

Two days after came the anniversary festival of the birth of Mahomet. At this Napoleon was also present, in company with the sheik El Bekri,[8] who at his request gave him two young Mamelukes, Ibrahim and Roustan.[9]

It has been alleged that Bonaparte, when in Egypt, took part in the

Bonaparte at the Festival of Muhamed in Cairo (Engraving by Colin)

Bonaparte and the
Pasha of Cairo

religious ceremonies and worship of the Mussulmans; but it cannot be said that he *celebrated* the festivals of the overflowing of the Nile and the anniversary of the Prophet. The Turks invited him to these merely as a spectator; and the presence of their new master was gratifying to the people. But he never committed the folly of ordering any solemnity. He neither learned nor repeated any prayer of the Koran, as many persons have asserted; neither did he advocate fatalism, polygamy, or any other doctrine of the Koran. Bonaparte employed himself better than in discussing with the Imaums the theology of the children of Ismael. The ceremonies, at which policy induced him to be present, were to him, and to all who accompanied him, mere matters of curiosity. He never set foot in a mosque; and only on one occasion, which I shall hereafter mention, dressed himself in the Mahometan costume. He attended the festivals to which the green turbans invited him.[10] His religious tolerance was the natural consequence of his philosophic spirit.

Doubtless Bonaparte did, as he was bound to do, show respect for the

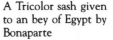

A Tricolor sash given to an bey of Egypt by Bonaparte

religion of the country; and he found it necessary to act more like a Mussulman than a Catholic. A wise conqueror supports his triumphs by protecting and even elevating the religion of the conquered people. Bonaparte's principle was, as he himself has often told me, to look upon religions as the work of men, but to respect them everywhere as a powerful engine of government. However, I will not go so far as to say that he would not have changed his religion had the conquest of the East been the price of that change. All that he said about Mahomet, Islamism, and the Koran to the great men of the country he laughed at himself. He enjoyed the gratification of having all his fine sayings on the subject of religion translated into Arabic poetry, and repeated from mouth to mouth. This of course tended to conciliate the people.

I confess that Bonaparte frequently conversed with the chiefs of the Mussulman religion on the subject of his conversion; but only for the sake of amusement. The priests of the Koran, who would probably have been delighted to convert us, offered us the most ample concessions. But these conversations were merely started by way of entertainment, and never could have warranted a supposition of their leading to any serious result. If Bonaparte spoke as a Mussulman, it was merely in his character of a military and political chief in a Mussulman country. To do so was essential to his success, to the safety of his army, and, consequently, to his glory. In every country he would have drawn up proclamations and delivered addresses on the same principle. In India he would have been for Ali, at Thibet for the Dalai-lama, and in China for Confucius.[11]

The General-in-Chief had a Turkish dress made, which he once put on, merely in joke. One day he desired me to go to breakfast without waiting for him, and that he would follow me. In about a quarter of an hour he made his appearance in his new costume. As soon as he was recognised, he was received with a loud burst of laughter. He sat down very coolly; but he found himself so encumbered and ill at ease in his turban and Oriental robe that he speedily threw them off, and was never tempted to a second performance of the masquerade.

About the end of August Bonaparte wished to open negotiations with the Pasha of Acre, nicknamed *the Butcher*. He offered Djezzar his friendship, sought his in return, and gave him the most consolatory assurances of the safety of his dominions. He promised to support him against the Grand Seignior, at the very moment when he was assuring the Egyptians that he would support the Grand Seignior against the beys. But Djezzar, confiding in his own strength and in the protection of the English, who had anticipated Bonaparte, was deaf to every overture, and would not even receive Beauvoisin, who was sent to him on the 22d of August. A second envoy was beheaded at Acre. The occupations of Bonaparte and the necessity of obtaining a more solid footing in Egypt retarded for the moment the invasion of that pashalic, which provoked vengeance by its barbarities, besides being a dangerous neighbour.

From the time he received the accounts of the disaster of Aboukir until the revolt of Cairo on the 22d of October, Bonaparte sometimes found the time hang heavily on his hands. Though he devoted attention to everything, yet there was not sufficient occupation for his singularly active mind. When the heat was not too great, he rode on horseback; and on his return, if he found no despatches to read (which often happened), no orders to send off, or no letters to answer, he was immediately absorbed in reverie, and would sometimes converse very strangely. One day, after a long pause, he said to me—

"Do you know what I am thinking of?"—"Upon my word, that would be very difficult; you think of such extraordinary things."—"I don't know," continued he, "that I shall ever see France again; but if I do, my only ambition is to make a glorious campaign in Germany—in the plains of Bavaria; there to gain a great battle, and to avenge France for the defeat of Hochstadt. After that I would retire into the country, and live quietly."

He then entered upon a long dissertation on the preference he would give to Germany as the theatre of war;[12] the fine character of the people, and the prosperity and wealth of the country, and its power of supporting an army. His conversations were sometimes very long, but always replete with interest.

In these intervals of leisure Bonaparte was accustomed to retire to bed early. I used to read to him every evening. When I read poetry, he would fall asleep; but when he asked for the "Life of Cromwell," I counted on sitting up pretty late. In the course of the day he used to read and make notes. He often expressed regret at not receiving news from France; for correspondence was rendered impracticable by the numerous English and Turkish cruisers. Many letters were intercepted and scandalously published. Not even family secrets and communications of the most confidential nature were respected.

About the middle of September in this year (1798), Bonaparte ordered to be brought to the house of Elfy Bey half a dozen Asiatic women whose beauty he had heard highly extolled. But their ungraceful obesity displeased him, and they were immediately dismissed. A few days after he fell violently in love with Madame Fourés, the wife of a lieutenant of infantry.[13] She was very pretty, and her charms were enhanced by the rarity of seeing a woman in Egypt who was calculated to please the eye of a European. Bonaparte engaged for her a house adjoining the palace of Elfy Bey, which we occupied. He frequently ordered dinner to be prepared there, and I used to go there with him at seven o'clock, and leave him at nine.

This connection soon became the general subject of gossip at headquarters. Through a feeling of *delicacy* to M. Fourés, the General-in-Chief gave him a mission to the Directory. He embarked at Alexandria, and the ship was captured by the English, who, being informed of the cause of his mission, were malicious enough to send him back to Egypt, instead of keeping him prisoner. Bonaparte wished to have a child by Madame Fourés, but this wish was not realised.

A celebrated soothsayer was recommended to Bonaparte by the inhabitants of Cairo, who confidentially vouched for the accuracy with which he

Oriental dancing girls

could foretell future events. He was sent for, and when he arrived, I, Venture, and a sheik were with the General. The prophet wished first to exercise his skill upon Bonaparte, who, however, proposed that I should have my fortune told first, to which I acceded without hesitation. To afford an idea of his prophetic skill I must mention that since my arrival in Cairo I had been in a very weak state. The passage of the Nile and the bad food we had had for twelve days had greatly reduced me, so that I was miserably pale and thin.

After examining my hands, feeling my pulse, my forehead, and the nape of my neck, the fortune-teller shrugged his shoulders, and, in a melancholy tone, told Venture that he did not think it right to inform me of my fate. I gave him to understand that he might say what he pleased, as it was a matter of indifference to me. After considerable hesitation on his part and pressing on mine, he announced to me that *the earth of Egypt would receive me in two months.*

I thanked him and he was dismissed. When we were alone, the General said to me, "Well, what do you think of that?" I observed that the fotune-teller did not run any great risk in foretelling my death, which was a very probable circumstance in the state in which I was; "but," added I, "if I procure the wines which I have ordered from France, you will soon see me get round again."

The art of imposing on mankind has at all times been an important part of the art of governing; and it was not that portion of the science of govern-

ment which Bonaparte was the least acquainted with. He neglected no opportunity of showing off to the Egyptians the superiority of France in arts and sciences; but it happened, oftener than once, that the simple instinct of the Egyptians thwarted his endeavours in this way. Some days after the visit of the pretended fortune-teller he wished, if I may so express myself, to oppose conjuror to conjuror. For this purpose he invited the principal sheiks to be present at some chemical experiments performed by M. Berthollet. The General expected to be much amused at their astonishment; but the miracles of the transformation of liquids, electrical commotions, and galvanism, did not elicit from them any symptom of surprise. They witnessed the operations of our able chemist with the most imperturbable indifference. When they were ended, the sheik El Bekri desired the interpreter to tell M. Berthollet that it was all very fine; "but," said he, "ask him whether he can make me be in Morocco and here at one and the same moment." M. Berthollet replied in the negative, with a shrug of his shoulders. "Oh, then," said the sheik, "he is not half a sorcerer."

Our music produced no greater effect upon them. They listened with insensibility to all the airs that were played to them, with the exception of "Marlbrook." When that was played, they became animated, and were all in motion, as if ready to dance.

An order which had been issued on our arrival in Cairo for watching the criers of the mosques had for some weeks been neglected. At certain hours of the night these criers address prayers to the Prophet. As it was merely a repetition of the same ceremony over and over again, in a short time no notice was taken of it. The Turks, perceiving this negligence, substituted for their prayers and hymns cries of revolt; and by this sort of verbal telegraph, insurrectionary excitement was transmitted to the northern and southern extremities of Egypt. By this means, and by the aid of secret emissaries, who eluded our feeble police, and circulated real or forged firmans of the Sultan disavowing the concern between France and the Porte, and provoking war, the plan of a revolution was organised throughout the country.

The signal for the execution of this plan was given from the minarets on the night of the 20th of October, and on the morning of the 21st it was announced at headquarters that the city of Cairo was in open insurrection. The General-in-Chief was not, as has been stated, in the isle of Raouddah: he did not hear the firing of the alarm-guns. He rose when the news arrived; it was then five o'clock. He was informed that all the shops were closed, and that the French were attacked. A moment after he heard of the death of General Dupuis, commandant of the garrison, who was killed by a lance in the street. Bonaparte immediately mounted his horse, and, accompanied by only thirty guides, visited all the threatened points, restored confidence, and, with great presence of mind, adopted measures of defence.

He left me at headquarters with only one sentinel; but he had been accurately informed of the situation of the insurgents; and such was my confidence in his activity and foresight that I had no apprehension, and awaited his return with perfect composure. This composure was not disturbed even when I saw a party of insurgents attack the house of M. Estève, our paymaster-general, which was situated on the opposite side of Ezbekye'h Place. M. Estève was, fortunately, able to resist the attack until troops from Boulac came up to his assistance.

After visiting all the posts, and adopting every precautionary measure, Bonaparte returned to headquarters. Finding me still alone with the sentinel, he asked me, smiling, "whether I had not been frightened?"—"Not at all, General, I assure you," replied I.

It was about half-past eight in the morning when Bonaparte returned to headquarters, and while at breakfast he was informed that some Bedouin Arabs, on horseback, was trying to force their entrance into Cairo. He ordered his aide-de-camp, Sulkowsky, to mount his horse, to take with him fifteen guides, and proceed to the point where the assailants were most numerous. This was the Bab-el-Nasser, or the gate of victory. Croisier observed to the General-in-Chief that Sulkowsky had scarcely recovered from the wounds at Salehye'h, and he offered to take his place. He had his motives for this. Bonaparte consented; but Sulkowsky had already set out. Within an hour after, one of the fifteen guides returned, covered with blood, to announce that Sulkowsky and the remainder of his party had been cut to pieces. This was speedy work, for we were still at table when the sad news arrived.

Mortars were planted on Mount Mokatam, which commands Cairo. The populace, expelled from all the principal streets by the troops, assembled in the square of the Great Mosque, and in the little streets running into it, which they barricaded. The firing of the artillery on the heights was kept up with vigour for two days.

Bonaparte pardoning revolutionaries of Cairo (Engraving by Raffet)

About twelve of the principal chiefs of Cairo were arrested and confined in an apartment at headquarters. They awaited with the calmest resignation the death they knew they merited; but Bonaparte merely detained them as hostages. The aga in the service of Bonaparte was astonished that sentence of death was not pronounced upon them; and he said, shrugging his shoulders, and with a gesture apparently intended to provoke severity, "You see they expect it."

On the third the insurrection was at an end, and tranquillity restored. Numerous prisoners were conducted to the citadel. In obedience to an order which I wrote every evening, twelve were put to death nightly. The bodies were then put into sacks and thrown into the Nile. There were many women included in these nocturnal executions. I am not aware that the number of victims amounted to thirty per day, as Bonaparte assured General Reynier in a letter which he wrote to him six days after the restoration of tranquillity. "Every night," said he, "we cut off thirty heads. This, I hope, will be an effectual example." I am of opinion that in this instance he exaggerated the extent of his just revenge.

Some time after the revolt of Cairo the necessity of insuring our own safety forced the commission of a terrible act of cruelty. A tribe of Arabs in the neighbourhood of Cairo had surprised and massacred a party of French. The General-in-Chief ordered his aide-de-camp Croisier to proceed to the spot, surround the tribe, destroy the huts, kill all the men, and conduct the rest of the population to Cairo. The order was to decapitate the victims, and bring their heads in sacks to Cairo to be exhibited to the people. Eugène Beauharnais accompanied Croisier, who joyfully set out on this horrible expedition, in hope of obliterating all recollection of the affair of Damanhour.

On the following day the party returned. Many of the poor Arab women had been delivered on the road, and the children had perished of hunger, heat, and fatigue. About four o'clock a troop of asses arrived in Ezbekye'h Place, laden with sacks. The sacks were opened, and the heads rolled out before the assembled populace. I cannot describe the horror I experienced; but I must nevertheless acknowledge that this butchery insured for a considerable time the tranquillity and even the existence of the little caravans which were obliged to travel in all directions for the service of the army.

Shortly before the loss of the fleet the General-in-Chief had formed the design of visiting Suez, to examine the traces of the ancient canal which united the Nile to the Gulf of Arabia, and also to cross the latter. The revolt at Cairo caused this project to be adjourned until the month of December.

Before his departure for Suez Bonaparte granted the commissary Sucy leave to return to France.[14] He had received a wound in the right hand when on board the xebec Cerf. I was conversing with him on deck when he received this wound. At first it had no appearance of being serious; but some time after he could not use his hand. General Bonaparte despatched a vessel with sick and wounded, who were supposed to be incurable, to the number of about eighty. All envied their fate and were anxious to depart with them; but the privilege was conceded to very few. However, those who were disappointed had no cause for regret. We never know what we wish for. Captain Marengo, who landed at Augusta in Sicily, supposing it to be a friendly land, was required to observe quarantine for twenty-two days, and information was given of the arrival of the vessel to the court, which was at Palermo. On the 25th of January, 1799, all on board the French vessel were massacred, with the exception of twenty-one, who were saved by a Neapolitan frigate, and conducted to Messina, where they were detained.

Before he conceived the resolution of attacking the Turkish advanced guard in the valleys of Syria, Bonaparte had formed a plan of invading British

India from Persia. He had ascertained, through the medium of agents, that the Shah of Persia would, for a sum of money paid in advance, consent to the establishment of military magazines on certain points of his territory. Bonaparte frequently told me that if, after the subjugation of Egypt, he could have left 15,000 men in that country, and have had 30,000 disposable troops, he would have marched on the Euphrates. He was frequently speaking about the deserts which were to be crossed to reach Persia.

How many times have I seen him extended on the ground, examining the beautiful maps which he had brought with him, and he would sometimes make me lie down in the same position to trace to me his projected march. This reminded him of the triumphs of his favourite hero, Alexander, with whom he so much desired to associate his name; but, at the same time, he felt that these projects were incompatible with our resources, the weakness of the Government, and the dissatisfaction which the army already evinced. Privation and misery are inseparable from all these remote operations.

This favourite idea still occupied his mind a fortnight before his departure for Syria was determined on, and on the 25th of January, 1799, he wrote to Tippoo Saib as follows:—

> "You are of course already informed of my arrival on the banks of the Red Sea, with a numerous and invincible army. Eager to deliver you from the iron yoke of England, I hasten to request that you will send me, by the way of Mascate or Mocha, an account of the political situation in which you are. I also wish that you could send to Suez, or Grand Cairo, some able man, in your confidence, with whom I may confer."[15]

Endnotes

*Memoirs of Napoleon Bonaparte by Louis Antoine Fauvelet de Bourrienne, in Four Volumes, (The Napoleon Society: Paris and Boston, 1895) Vol. I, pp 158–191.

[1] Some idea of the misery endured by the French troops on this occasion may be gathered from the following description in Napoleon's "Memoirs," dictated at St. Helena:—

"As the Hebrews, wandering in the wilderness, complained, and angrily asked Moses for the onions and flesh-pots of Egypt, the French soldiers constantly regretted the luxuries of Italy. In vain were they assured that the country was the most fertile in the world, that it was even superior to Lombardy; how were they to be persuaded of this when they could get neither bread nor wine? We encamped on immense quantities of wheat, but there was neither mill nor oven in the country. The biscuit brought from Alexandria had long been exhausted; the soldiers were even reduced to bruise the wheat between two stones and to make cakes, which they baked under the ashes. Many parched the wheat in a pan, after which they boiled it. This was the best way to use the grain; but after all, it was not bread. The apprehensions of the soldiers increased daily, and rose to such a pitch that a great number of them said there was no great city of Cairo; and that the place bearing the name was, like Damanhour, a vast assemblage of mere huts, destitute of everything that could render life comfortable or agreeable. To such a melancholy state of mind had they brought themselves that two dragoons threw themselves, completely clothed, into the Nile, where they were drowned. It is nevertheless true that, though there was neither bread nor wine, the resources which were procured with wheat, lentils, meat, and sometimes pigeons, furnished the army with food of some kind. But the evil was in the ferment of the mind. The officers complained more loudly than the soldiers, because the comparison was proportionately more disadvantaged to them. In Egypt they found neither the quarters, the good table, nor the luxury of Italy. The General-in-Chief, wishing to set an example, used to bivouac in the midst of the army, and in the least commodious spots. No one had either tent or provisions; the dinner of Napoleon and his staff consisted of a dish of lentils. The soldiers passed the evenings in political conversations, arguments, and complaints. 'For what purpose are we come here?' said some of them; 'the Directory has transported us.' 'Caffarelli,' said others, 'is the agent that has been made use of to deceive the General-in-Chief.' Many of them, having observed that wherever there were vestiges of antiquity they were carefully searched, vented their spite in invective against the *savants*, or scientific men, who, they said, *had started the idea of the expedition in order to make these searches.* Jests were showered upon them, even in their presence. The men called an ass a *savant*, and said of Caffarelli Dufalga, alluding to his wooden leg, 'He laughs at all these troubles; he has one foot in France.'"

[2] Bonaparte had great confidence in him. He had commanded, under the General's orders, the naval forces in the Adriatic in 1797.—*Bourrienne*.

[3] Bonaparte's autograph note, after enumerating the troops and warlike stores he wished to be sent, concluded with the following list:—

1st, a company of actors; 2d, a company of dancers; 3d, some dealers in marionettes, at least three or four; 4th, a hundred French women; 5th, the wives of all the men employed in the corps; 6th, twenty surgeons, thirty apothecaries, and ten physicians; 7th, some founders; 8th, some distillers and dealers in liquor; 9th, fifty gardeners with their families, and the seeds of every kind of vegetable; 10th, each party to bring with them 200,000 pints of brandy; 11th, 30,000 ells of blue and scarlet cloth; 12th, a supply of soap and oil.—*Bourrienne*.

[4] Far more thoroughly and actively than those taken by the English Government in 1882–3–4!

[5] "*Bourrienne et ses Erreurs, Volontairs* et *Involontaires*." Edited by Compte d'Aure (Parris, Heideloff, 1830)."Erreurs" objects to this description of the complaints of the army, but Savary (tome i, pp. 56, 57, and tome i, p. 89) fully confirms it, giving the reason that the army was not a homogeneous body, but a mixed force taken from Rome, Florence, Milan, Venice, Genoa, and Marseilles; see also Thiers, tome v. p. 283. But the fact is not singular. For a striking instance, in the days of the Empire, of the soldiers in 1809, in Spain, actually threatening Napoleon in his own hearing, see De Gonneville (tome i. pp. 190–193); "The soldiers of Lapisse's division gave loud expression to the most sinister designs against the Emperor's person, stirring up each other to fire a shot at him, and bandying accusations of cowardice for not doing it. He heard it all as plainly as we did, and seemed as if he did not care a bit for it, but" sent the division into good quarters, when the men were as enthusiastic as they were formerly mutinous. In 1796 D'Entraigues, the Bourbon spy, reports, "As a general rule, the French soldier grumbles and is discontented. He accuses Bonaparte of being a thief and a rascal. But to-morrow the very same soldier will obey him blindly" (Iung's *Bonaparte*, tome iii, p. 152).

[6] Napoleon related at St. Helena that in a fit of irritation he rushed among the group of dissatisfied generals, and said to one of them, who was remarkable for his stature, "You have held seditious language; but take care I do not perform my duty. Though you are five feet ten inches high, that shall not save you from being shot."—*Bourrienne*.

[7] The Institute of Egypt was composed of members of the French Institute, and of the men of science and artists of the commission who did not belong to that body. They assembled and added to their number several officers of the artillery and staff, and others who had cultivated the sciences and literature.

The Institute was established in one of the palaces of the beys. A great number of machines, and physical, chemical, and astronomical instruments had been brought from France. They were distributed in the different rooms, which were also successively filled with all the curiosities of the country, whether of the animal, vegetable, or mineral kingdom.

The garden of the palace became a botanical garden. A chemical laboratory was formed at headquarters; Berthollet performed experiments there several times every week, at which Napoleon and a great number of officers attended *(Memoirs of Napoleon)*.

[8]The General-in-Chief went to celebrate the feast of the Prophet at the house of the sheik El Bekri. The ceremony was begun by the recital of a kind of litany, containing the life of Mahomet from his birth to his death. About a hundred sheiks, sitting in a circle, on carpets, with their legs crossed, recited all the verses, swinging their bodies violently backwards and forwards, and all together.

A grand dinner was afterwards served up, at which the guests sat on carpets, with their legs across. There were twenty tables, and five or six people at each table. That of the General-in-Chief and the sheik El Bekri was in the middle; a little slab of a precious kind of wood ornamented with mosaic-work was placed eighteen inches above the floor and covered with a great number of dishes in succession. They were pillaws of rice, a particular kind of roast, *entrées,* and pastry, all very highly spiced. The sheiks picked everything with their fingers. Accordingly, water was brought to wash the hands three times during dinner. Gooseberry-water, lemonade, and other sorts of sherbets were served to drink, and abundance of preserves and confectionery with the dessert. On the whole, the dinner was not disagreeable, it was only the manner of eating it that seemed strange to us.

In the evening the whole city was illuminated. After dinner the party went into the square of El Bekri, the illumination of which, in coloured lamps, was very beautiful. An immense concourse of people attended. They were all placed in order, in ranks of from twenty to a hundred persons, who, standing close together, recited the prayers and litanies of the Prophet with movements which kept increasing, until at length they seemed to be convulsive, and some of the most zealous fainted away *(Memoirs of Napoleon)*.

[9]Roustan or Rustan, a Mameluke, was always with Napoleon from the time of the return from Egypt till 1814, when he abandoned his master. He slept at or near the door of Napoleon. See Rémusat, tome i, p. 209, for an amusing description of the alarm of Josephine, and the precipitate flight of Madame de Rémusat, at the idea of being met and killed by this man in one of Josephine's nocturnal attacks on the privacy of her husband when closeted with his mistress.

[10]From this Sir Walter Scott infers that he did not scruple to join the Mussulmans in the external ceremonies of their religion. He embellishes his romance with the ridiculous farce of the sepulchral chamber of the grand pyramid, and the speeches which were addressed to the General as well as to the muftis and Imaums; and he adds that Bonaparte was on the point of embracing Islamism. All that Sir Walter says on this subject is the height of absurdity, and does not even deserve to be seriously refuted. Bonaparte never entered a mosque except from motives of curiosity, and he never for one moment afforded any ground for supposing that he *believed in the mission of Mahomet.—Bourrienne.*

[11]On the subject of his alleged conversion to Mahometanism, Bonaparte expressed himself at St. Helena as follows:—

"I never followed any of the tenets of that religion. I never prayed in the mosques. I never abstained from wine, or was circumcised, neither did I ever profess it. I said merely that we were the friends of the Mussulmans, and that I respected Mahomet their Prophet, which was true; I respect him now. I wanted to make the Imaums cause prayers to be offered up in the mosques for me, in order to make the people respect me still more than they actually did, and obey me more readily. The Imaums replied that there was a great obstacle, because their Prophet in the Koran had inculcated to them that they were not to obey, respect, or hold faith with infidels, and that I came under that denomination. I then desired them to hold a consultation, and see what was necessary to be done in order to become a Mussulman, as some of their tenets could not be practised by us. That, as to circumcision, God had made us unfit for that. That, with respect to drinking wine, we were poor cold people, inhabitants of the north, who could not exist without it. They consulted together accordingly, and in about three weeks issued a fetham, declaring that circumcision might be omitted, because it was merely a profession; that as to drinking wine, it might be drunk by Mussulmans, but that those who drank it would not go to paradise, but to hell. I replied that this would not do; that we had no occasion to make ourselves Mussulmans in order to go to hell; that there were many ways of getting there without coming to Egypt, and desired them to hold another consultation. After deliberating and battling together for I believe three months, they finally decided that a man might become a Mussulman, and neither circumcise nor abstain from wine; but that, in proportion to the wine drunk, some good works must be done. I then told them that we were all Mussulmans and friends of the Prophet, which they really believed, as the French soldiers never went to church, and had no priests with them. For you must know that during the Revolution there was no religion whatever in the French army. Menou," continued Napoleon, "really turned Mahometan, which was the reason I left him behind."—*Voice from St. Helena.*

[12]So early as 1794 Napoleon had suggested that Austria should always be attacked in Germany, not in Italy. "It is Germany that should be overwhelmed; that done, Italy and Spain fall of themselves. . . . Germany should be attacked, not Spain or Italy. If we obtain great success, advantage should never be taken of it to penetrate into Italy while Germany, unweakened, offers a formidable front" (Iung's *Bonparte,* tome ii, p. 436). He was always opposed to the wild plans which had ruined so many French armies in Italy, and which the Directory tried to force on him, of marching on Rome and Naples after every success in the north.

[13]See "Memoirs of the Duchesse d'Abrantès" (Madame Junot), Engish edition of 1883, vol. i, p. 458.

[14]"Erreurs" (tome i, p. 67) says that the expedition to Suez started in Nivôse (December and January), and that Sucy had gone home three months before.

[15]It is not true, as has often been stated, that Tippoo Saib wrote to General Bonaparte. He could not reply to a letter written on the 25th of January, owing to the great difficulty of communication, the considerable distance, and the short interval which elapsed between the 25th of January and the fall of the empire of Mysore, which happened on the 20th of April following. The letter addressed to Tippoo Saib commenced, "Citizen-Sultan!"—*Bourrienne.*

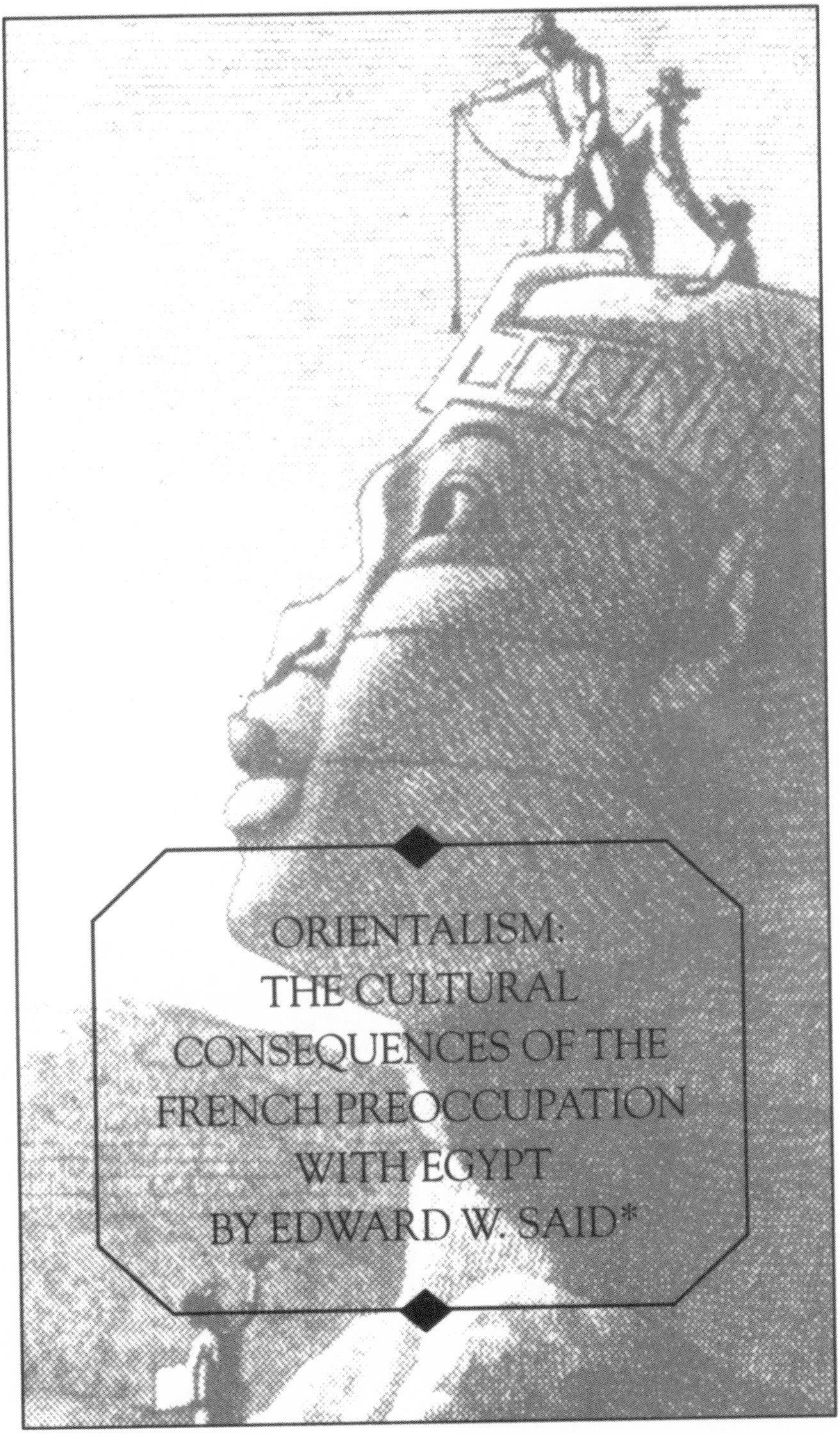

ORIENTALISM: THE CULTURAL CONSEQUENCES OF THE FRENCH PREOCCUPATION WITH EGYPT

BY EDWARD W. SAID*

Napoleon's enlistment of several dozen "savants" for his Egyptian Expedition is too well known to require detail here. His idea was to build a sort of living archive for the expedition, in the form of studies conducted on all topics by the members of the Institut d'Égypte, which he founded. What is perhaps less well known is Napoleon's prior reliance upon the work of the Comte de Volney, a French traveler whose *Voyage en Égypte et en Syrie* appeared in two volumes in 1787. Aside from a short personal preface informing the reader that the sudden acquisition of some money (his inheritance) made it possible for him to take the trip east in 1783, Volney's *Voyage* is an almost oppressively impersonal document. Volney evidently saw himeself as a scientist, whose job it was always to record the "état" of something he saw. The climax of the *Voyage* occurs in the second volume, an account of Islam as a religion.[1] Volney's views were canonically hostile to Islam as a religion and as a system of political institutions; nevertheless Napoleon found this work and Volney's *Considérations sur la guerre actuel de Turcs* (1788) of particular importance. For Volney after all was a canny Frenchman, and—like Chateaubriand and Lamartine a quarter-century after him—he eyed the Near Orient as a likely place for the realization of French colonial ambition. What Napoleon profited from in Volney was the enumeration, in ascending order of difficulty, of the obstacles to be faced in the Orient by any French expeditionary force.

Napoleon refers explicitly to Volney in his reflections on the Egyptian expedition, the *Campagnes d'Égypte et de Syrie, 1798–1799*, which he dictated to General Bertrand on Saint Helena. Volney, he said, considered that there were three barriers to French hegemony in the Orient and that any French force would therefore have to fight three wars: one against England, a second against the Ottoman Porte, and a third, the most difficult, against the Muslims.[2] Volney's assessment was both shrewd and hard to fault since it was clear to Napoleon, as it would be to anyone who read Volney, that his *Voyage* and the *Considérations* were effective texts to be used by the

European wishing to win in the Orient. In other words, Volney's work constituted a handbook for attenuating the human shock a European might feel as he directly experienced the Orient: Read the books, seems to have been Volney's thesis, and far from being disoriented by the Orient, you will compel it to you.

Napoleon took Volney almost literally, but in a characteristically subtle way. From the first moment that the Armée d'Égypte appeared on the Egyptian horizon, every effort was made to convince the Muslims that "nous sommes les vrais musulmans," as Bonapate's proclamation of July 2, 1798, put it to the people of Alexandria.[3] Equipped with a team of Orientalists (and sitting on board a flagship called the *Orient*), Napoleon used Egyptian enmity towards the Mamelukes and appeals to the revolutionary idea of equal opportunity for all to wage a uniquely benign and selective war against Islam. What more than anything impressed the first Arab chronicler of the expedition, Abd-al-Rahman al-Jabartī, was Napoleon's use of scholars to manage his contacts with the natives—that and the impact of watching a modern European intellectual establishment at close quarters.[4] Napoleon tried everywhere to prove that he was fighting *for* Islam; everything he said was translated into Koranic Arabic, just as the French army was urged by its command always to remember the Islamic sensibility. (Compare, in this regard, Napoleon's tactics in Egypt with the tactics of the *Requerimiento,* a document drawn up in 1513—in Spanish—by the Spaniards to be read aloud to the Indians: "We shall take you and your wives and your children, and shall make slaves of them, and as such sell and dispose of them as their Highnesses [the King and Queen of Spain] may command; and we shall take away your goods, and shall do you all the mischief and damage that we can, as to vassals who do not obey," etc. etc.[5]) When it seemed obvious to Napoleon that his force was too small to impose itself on the Egyptians, he then tried to make the local imams, cadis, muftis, and ulemas interpret the Koran in favor of the Grande Armée. To this end, the sixty ulemas who taught at the Azhar were invited to his quarters, given full military honors, and then allowed to be flattered by Napoleon's admiration for Islam and Mohammed and by his obvious veneration for the Koran, with which he seemed perfectly familiar. This worked, and soon the population of Cairo seemed to have lost its distrust of the occupiers.[6] Napoleon later gave his deputy Kleber strict instructions after he left always to administer Egypt through the Orientalists and the religious Islamic leaders whom they could win over; any other politics was too expensive and foolish.[7] Hugo thought that he grasped the tactful glory of Napoleon's Oriental expedition in his poem "Lui":

Au nil je le retrouve encore.
L'Égypte resplendit des feux de son aurore;
Son astre impérial se lève à l'orient.
Vainqueur, enthousiaste, éclatant de prestiges,
Prodige, il étonna la terre des prodiges.
Les vieux scheiks vénéraient l'émir jeune et prudent;
Le peuple redoutait ses armes inouïes;
Sublime, il apparut aux tribus éblouies
Comme un Mahomet d'occident.[8]

(By the Nile, I find him once again.
Egypt shines with the fires of his dawn;
His imperial orb rises in the Orient.

Victor, enthusiast, bursting with achievements,
Prodigious, he stunned the land of prodigies.
The old sheikhs venerated the young and prudent emir.
The people dreaded his unprecedented arms;
Sublime, he appeared to the dazzled tribes
Like a Mahomet of the Occident.)

Such a triumph could only have been prepared *before* a military expedition, perhaps only by someone who had no prior experience of the Orient except what books and scholars told him. The idea of taking along a full-scale academy is very much an aspect of this textual attitude to the Orient. And this attitude in turn was bolstered by specific Revolutionary decrees (particularly the one of 10 Germinal An III—March 30, 1793—establishing an *école publique* in the Bibliothèque nationale to teach Arabic, Turkish, and Persian)[9] whose object was the rationalist one of dispelling mystery and institutionalizing even the most recondite knowledge. Thus many of Napoleon's Orientalist translators were students of Sylvestre de Sacy, who, beginning in June 1796, was the first and only teacher of Arabic at the École publique des langues orientales. Sacy later became the teacher of nearly every major Orientalist in Europe, where his students dominated the field for about three-quarters of a century. Many of them were politically useful, in the ways that several had been to Napoleon in Egypt.

But dealings with the Muslims were only a part of Napoleon's project to dominate Egypt. The other part was to render it completely open, to make it totally accessible to European scrutiny. From being a land of obscurity and a part of the Orient hitherto known at second hand through the exploits of

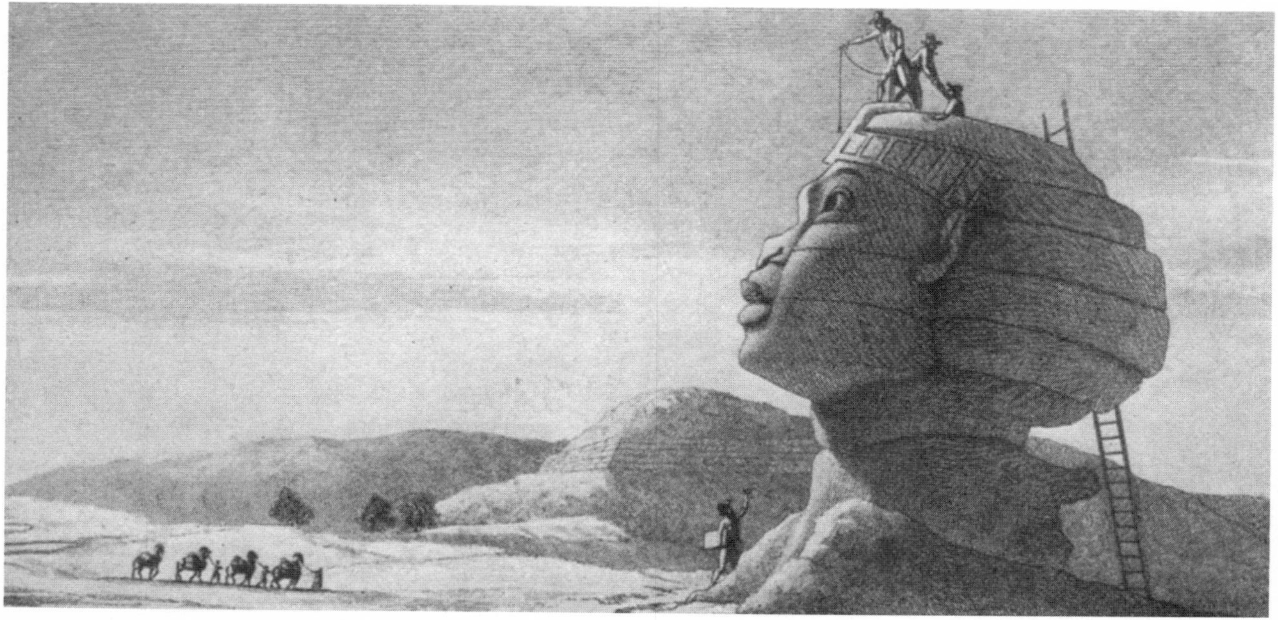

French scholars measuring the sphinx

earlier travelers, scholars, and conquerors, Egypt was to become a department of French learning. Here too the textual and schematic attitudes are evident. The Institut, with its teams of chemists, historians, biologists, archaeologists, surgeons, and antiquarians, was the learned division of the army. Its job was no less aggressive: to put Egypt into modern French; and unlike the Abbé Le Mascrier's 1735 *Description de l'Égypte*, Napoleon's was to be a universal undertaking. Almost from the first moments of the occupation Napoleon saw to it that the Institut began its meetings, its experiments—its fact-finding mission, as we would call it today. Most important, everything said, seen, and studied was to be recorded, and indeed was recorded in that great collective appropriation of one country by another, the *Description de l'Égypte*, published in twenty-three enormous volumes between 1809 and 1828.[10]

The *Description*'s uniqueness is not only in its size, or even in the intelligence of its contributors, but in its attitude to its subject matter, and it is this attitude that makes it of great interest for the study of modern Orientalist projects. The first few pages of its *préface historique*, written by Jean-Baptiste-Joseph Fourier, the Institut's secretary, make it clear that in "doing" Egypt the scholars were also grappling directly with a kind of unadulterated cultural, geographical, and historical significance. Egypt was the focal point of the relationships between Africa and Asia, between Europe and the East, between memory and actuality.

> Placed between Africa and Asia, and communicating easily with Europe, Egypt occupies the center of the ancient continent. This country presents only great memories; it is the homeland of the arts and conserves innumerable monuments; its principal temples and the palaces inhabited by its kings still exist, even though its least ancient edifices had already been built by the time of the Trojan War. Homer, Lycurgus, Solon, Pythagoras, and Plato all went to Egypt to study the sciences, religion, and the laws. Alexander founded an opulent city there, which for a long time enjoyed commercial supremacy and which witnessed Pompey, Caesar, Mark Antony, and Augustus deciding between them the fate of Rome and that of the entire world. It is therefore proper for this country to attract the attention of illustrious princes who rule the destiny of nations.
>
> No considerable power was ever amassed by any nation, whether in the West or in Asia, that did not also turn that nation toward Egypt, which was regarded in some measure as its natural lot.[11]

Because Egypt was saturated with meaning for the arts, sciences, and government, its role was to be the stage on which actions of a world-historical importance would take place. By taking Egypt, then, a modern power would naturally demonstrate its strength and justify history; Egypt's own destiny was to be annexed, to Europe preferably. In addition, this power would also enter a history whose common element was defined by figures no less great than Homer, Alexander, Caesar, Plato, Solon, and Pythagoras, who graced the Orient with their prior presence there. The Orient, in short, existed as a set of values attached, not to its modern realities, but to a series of valorized contacts it had had with a distant European past. This is a pure example of the textual, schematic attitude I have been referring to.

Fourier continues similarly for over a hundred pages (each page, incidentally, is a square meter in size, as if the project and the size of the page had been thought of as possessing comparable scale). Out of the free-floating past, however, he must justify the Napoleonic expedition as something that needed to be undertaken when it happened. The dramatic perspective is never abandoned. Conscious of his European audience and of the Oriental figures he was manipulating, he writes:

> One remember the impression made on the whole of Europe by the astounding news that the French were in the Orient. . . . This great project was mediated in silence, and was prepared with such activity and secrecy that the worried vigilance of our enemies was deceived; only at the moment that it happened did they learn that it had been conceived, undertaken, and carried out successfully. . . .

So dramatic a *coup de théâtre* had its advantages for the Orient as well:

> This country, which has transmitted its knowledge to so many nations, is today plunged into barbarism.

Only a hero could bring all these factors together, which is what Fourier now describes:

> Napoleon appreciated the influence that this event would have on the relations between Europe, the Orient, and Africa, on Mediterranean shipping, and on Asia's destiny. . . . Napoleon wanted to offer a useful European example to the Orient, and finally also to make the inhabitants' lives more pleasant, as well as to procure for them all the advantages of a perfected civilization.
>
> None of this would be possible without a continuous application to the project of the arts and sciences.[12]

To restore a region from its present barbarism to its former classical greatness; to instruct (for its own benefit) the Orient in the ways of the modern West; to subordinate or underplay military power in order to aggrandize the

Frontispiece of "Description de l'Egypte" published under the auspices of General Kléber
(Drawing by Létile, architect in the Armée d'Orient)

Explorations by the Institut d'Egypte

project of glorious knowledge acquired in the process of political domination of the Orient; to formulate the Orient, to give it shape, identity, definition with full recognition of its place in memory, its importance to imperial strategy, and its "natural" role as an appendage to Europe; to dignify all the knowledge collected during colonial occupation with the title "contribution to modern learning" when the natives had neither been consulted nor treated as anything except as pretexts for a text whose usefulness was not to the natives; to feel oneself as a European in command, almost at will, of Oriental history, time, and geography; to institute new areas of specialization; to establish new disciplines; to divide, deploy, schematize, tabulate, index, and record everything in sight (and out of sight); to make out of every observable detail a generalization and out of every generalization an immutable law about the Oriental nature, temperament, mentality, custom, or type; and, above all, to transmute living reality into the stuff of texts, to possess (or think one possesses) actuality mainly because nothing in the Orient seems to resist one's powers: these are the features of Orientalist projection entirely realized in the *Description de l'Égypte,* itself enabled and reinforced by Napoleon's wholly Orientalist engulfment of Egypt by the instruments of Western knowledge and power. Thus Fourier concludes his preface by announcing that history will remember how "Égypte fut le théâtre de sa [Napoleon's] gloire, et préserve de l'oubli toutes les circonstances de cet évènement extraordinaire."[13]

The *Description* thereby displaces Egyptian or Oriental history as a history possessing its own coherence, identity, and sense. Instead, history as recorded in the *Description* supplants Egyptian or Oriental history by identifying itself directly and immediately with world history, a euphemism for European history. To save an event from oblivion is in the Orientalist's mind the equivalent of turning the Orient into a theater for his representations of the Orient: this is almost exactly what Fourier says. Moreover, the sheer power of having described the Orient in modern Occidental terms lifts the Orient from the realms of silent obscurity where it has lain neglected (except for the inchoate murmurings of a vast but undefined sense of its own past) into the clarity of modern European science. There this new Orient figures as—for instance, in Geoffroy Saint-Hilaire's biological theses in the *Description*—the confirmation of laws of zoological specialization formulated by Buffon.[14] Or it serves as a "contraste frappante avec les habitudes des nations Européenes,"[15] in which the "bizarre jouissances" of Orientals serve to highlight the sobriety and rationality of Occidental habits. Or, to cite one more use for the Orient, equivalent of those Oriental physiological characteristics that made possible the successful embalming of bodies are sought for in European bodies, so that chevaliers fallen on the field of honor can be preserved as lifelike relics of Napoleon's great Oriental campaign.[16]

Yet the military failure of Napoleon's occupation of Egypt did not also destroy the fertility of its over-all projection for Egypt or the rest of the

Orient. Quite literally, the occupation gave birth to the entire modern experience of the Orient as interpreted from within the universe of discourse founded by Napoleon in Egypt, whose agencies of domination and dissemination included the Institut and the *Description.* The idea, as it has been characterized by Charles-Roux, was that Egypt "restored to prosperity, regenerated by wise and enlightened administration . . . would shed its civilizing rays upon all its Oriental neighbors."[17] True, the other European powers would seek to compete in this mission, none more than England. But what would happen as a continuing legacy of the common Occidental mission to the Orient—despite inter-European squabbling, indecent competition, or outright war—would be the creation of new projects, new visions, new enterprises combining additional parts of the old Orient with the conquering European spirit. After Napoleon, then, the very language of Orientalism changed radically. Its descriptive realism was upgraded and became not merely a style of representation but a language, indeed a means of *creation.* Along with the *langues mères,* as those forgotten dormant sources for the modern European demotics were entitled by Antoine Fabre d'Olivet, the Orient was reconstructed, reassembled, crafted, in short, *born* out of the Orientalists' efforts. The *Description* became the master type of all further efforts to bring the Orient closer to Europe, thereafter to absorb it entirely and—centrally important—to cancel, or at least subdue and reduce, its strangeness and, in the case of Islam, its hostility. For the Islamic Orient would henceforth appear as a category denoting the Orientalists' power and not the Islamic people as humans nor their history as history.

Thus out of the Napoleonic expedition there issued a whole series of textual children, from Chateaubriand's *Itinéraire* to Lamartine's *Voyage en Orient* to Flaubert's *Salammbô*, and in the same tradition, Lane's *Manners and Customs of the Modern Egyptians* and Richard Burton's *Personal Narrative of a Pilgrimage to al-Madinan and Meccah.* What binds them together is not only their common background in Oriental legend and experience but also their learned reliance on the Orient as a kind of womb out of which they were brought forth. If paradoxically these creations turned out to be highly stylized simulacra, elaborately wrought imitations of what a live Orient might be thought to look like, that by no means detracts either from the strength of their imaginative conception or from the strength of European mastery of the Orient, whose prototypes respectively were Cagliostro, the great European impersonator of the Orient, and Napoleon, its first modern conqueror.

Bonaparte inaugurating the Institut d'Egypte in the palace of Ḥasan Kāshif in Cairo (Drawing by Protain)

Endnotes

*From "Orientalism" by Edward W. Said, Panteon Books. 1978, pp. 81–88.

[1] Constantin-François Volney, *Voyage en Égypte et eu Syrie* (Paris: Bossange, 1821), 2: 241 and passim.

[2] Napoleon, *Campagnes d'Égypte et de Syrie, 1798–1799: Mémoires pour servir à l'histoire de Napoléon* (Paris: Comou, 1843), 1: 211.

[3] Thiry, *Bonaparte en Égypte,* p. 126. See also Ibrahim Abu-Lughod, *Arab Rediscovery of Europe: A Study in Cultural Encounters* (Princeton, N.J.: Princeton University Press, 1963), pp. 12–20.

[4] Abu-Lughod, *Arab Rediscovery of Europe,* p. 22.

[5] Quoted from Arthur Helps, *The Spanish Conquest of America* (London, 1900), p. 196, by Stephen J. Greenblatt, "Learning to Curse: Aspects of Linguistic Colonialism in the Sixteenth Century," in *First Images of America: The Impact of the New World on the Old,* ed. Fredi Chiapelli (Berkeley: University of California Press, 1976), p. 573.

[6] Thiry, *Bonaparte en Égypte,* p. 200. Napoleon was not just being cynical. It is reported of him that he discussed Voltaire's *Mahomet* with Goethe, and defended Islam. See Christian Cherfils, *Bonaparte et l'Islam d'après les documents français arabes* (Paris: A. Pedone, 1914), p. 249 and passim.

[7] Thiry, *Bonaparte en Égypte,* p. 434.

[8] Hugo, *Les Orientales,* in *Oeuvres poétiques,* 1: 684.

[9] Henri Dehéraine, *Silvestre de Sacy, ses contemporains et ses disciples* (Paris: Paul Geuthner, 1938), p. v.

[10] *Description de l'Égypte, ou Recueil des observations et des recherches qui ont été faites in Égypte pendant l'expédition de l'armée française, publié par les ordres de sa majesté l'empereur Napoléon le grand,* 23 vols. (Paris: Imprimerie impériale, 1809–28).

[11] Fourier, *Préface historique,* vol. 1 of *Description de l'Égypte,* p. 1.

[12] Ibid., p. iii.

[13] Ibid., p. xcii.

[14] Etienne Geoffroy Saint-Hilaire, *Histoire naturelle des poissons du Nil,* vol. 17 of *Description de l'Égypte*, p. 2.

[15] M. de Chabrol, *Essai sur les moeurs des habitants modernes de l'Égypte,* vol. 14 of *Description de l'Égypte,* p. 376.

[16] This is evident in Baron Larrey, *Notice sur la conformation physique des égyptiens et des différeutes vaces quí habiteut en Égypte, suivie de quelques réflexions sur l'em baumement des momies*, vol. 13 of *Descriptions de l'Égypte.*

[17] Cited by John Marlowe, *The Making of the Suez Canal* (London: Cresset Press, 1964), p. 31.

ABOUT THE CONTRIBUTORS

'ABD AL-RAḤMĀN AL-JABARTĪ (1187/1753–1241/1825)[1] was an Egyptian scholar, historian, and biographer, the son of the eminent scholar Ḥasan al-Jabartī (1109/1697–1188/1774), who excelled in mathematics, geometry, algebra, astronomy and Islamic philosophy. Some of his works are extant as published books and manuscripts. His son 'Abd al-Raḥmān, the only survivor of his father's forty children, followed in his footsteps. 'Abd al-Raḥmān al-Jabartī pursued research in the sciences, especially medicine and arithmetic. However, the history of Egypt was his main concern, and he wrote three works on the subject. The first, which is untitled, given by one of its owners the title *Tārīkh muddat al-Faransīs bi-Miṣr,* depicts the first seven months of the French occupation of Egypt, from Muḥharram to Rajab 1213 (June 15 to December, 1798); it was written in 1798 under the immediate impression of the events of the French occupation.[2] The second book, entitled *Maẓhar al-Taqdīs bi-Zawāl Dawlat al-Faransīs,* deals with the French occupation between June 15 and the end of December 1801 (Sha'bān 1216).[3] The final work on Egyptian history is his comprehensive *'Ajā'ib al-Āthār fi 'l-Tarājīm wa'l-Akhbār,* written in two versions. The first comprises three volumes, covering the period between 1100/1688–89 to 1221/1806).[4] The second version follows the first one until the first third of the third volume (Ramaḍān, 1214/1799–1800), to which the author added details on the events up to 1806. He also added a fourth volume to his history, which covers events from 1807 to 1821, and intended to supplement it with a fifth volume.[5]

In writing *'Ajā'ib al-Āthār,* al-Jabartī included information which he could verify from elderly witnesses, registers, tombstones and chronicles such as Aḥmad Shalabī b. 'Abd al-Ghanī, *Awḍaḥ al-Ishārāt fī Man Tawallā Miṣr al Qāhira min al-Wuzarā' wa-'l-Bāshāt* (1715–1755), and al-Damurdāshī, *al-Durra al-Musāna fī Akhbār al-Kināna* (1668–1755).[6] We may presume that the invitation of the Damascene historian, al-Murādī (1760–1791), to Murtaḍā al-Zabīdī (1732–1790) and al-Jabartī to cooperate with him in collecting biographical data provided him with the primary impulse to write a history of Egypt. The second impulse came from the unusual events surrounding the French occupation of Egypt, on which he recorded his *Tārīkh Muddat āl-Faransīs*. *Maẓhar al-Taqdīs* was written in order to clear himself of the accusation of cooperation with the French, because he was a member of the third Dīwān which the French had insisted to be formed to govern Egypt. The success of Maẓhar gave him the final impulse to write his *'Ajā'ib al-Āthār* in 1220–21/1805–6. This chronicle is considered the best account of Egyptian history between the 17th and 19th centuries.

Al-Jabarti is the first herald of the Arab renaissance who opposed popular Sufism and superstition. At the first shock of the French occupation of Egypt, he accused the French of being "materialists who deny all God's attributes, the Hereafter and the Resurrection, and who reject Prophethood. . . ."[7] He can be considered the first Arab thinker aware of the modern spirit of the French revolution and the Napoleonic era and its slogans liberty, equality, and fraternity.

After the expulsion of the French from Egypt and the return of the Ottomans, he expressed his appreciation of European scientific, moral and technical achievement in *'Ajā'ib*. He admitted, after attending chemical and physical experiments by French scientists, that "these are things that the minds of people like us cannot grasp" ('Ajā'ib, III, 36, lines 6–7). On the other hand he accused the Ottoman soldiers of having no respect for human life, while the French had given a fair trial to Sulaymān al-Ḥalabī, General Jacques Menou's killer, even though he was caught with his knife in his hand.

His awareness of the shortcomings of the Muslim nations in his time predates the demand of the later generation of Muslim reformers for a return to the original sublime Islamic morals, customs, and beliefs, and for a scientific revival in the Arab world. Al-Jabartī's comments confirm that the real renaissance began with the French occupation of Egypt and not only through Ottoman reforms and the internal dynamics of the Arab world.

According to Mahmūd al-Sharqāwī, the attacks of al-Jabartī on Muḥammad 'Alī, the new ruler of Egypt, in the fifth volume of *'Ajā'ib*, caused the volume to be confiscated and his son to be killed in punishment.[8]

After this tragedy al-Jabarti, blind, stopped writing his chronicle, confining himself to his house, until he died from grief in 1241/1825.

S. Moreh,
Jerusalem, January, 1993

Louis Antoine Fauvelet de Bourrienne was born in 1769, that is, in the same year as Napoleon Bonaparte, and he was the friend and companion of the future Emperor at the military school of Brienne-le-Château till 1784, when Napoleon attended the Military School of Paris. The friends again met in 1792 and in 1795, when Napoleon was hanging about Paris, and when Bourrienne looked on the vague dreams of his old schoolmate as only so much folly. In 1796, as soon as Napoleon had assured his position at the head of the army of Italy, anxious as ever to surround himself with known faces, he sent for Bourrienne to be his secretary. Bourrienne had been appointed in 1792 as secretary of the Legation at Stuttgart, and returned to Paris in 1795. He joined Napoleon in 1797, after the Austrians had been beaten out of Italy, and at once assumed the office of secretary which he held for quite a long time.

He went with his General to Egypt, and returned with him to France. While Napoleon was making his formal entry into the Tuileries, Bourrienne was preparing the cabinet he was still to share with the Consul. In this cabinet—*our* cabinet, as he is careful to call it—he worked with the First Consul till 1802.

During all this time the pair had lived on terms of equality and friendship creditable to both. The secretary neither asked for nor received any salary: when he required money, he simply dipped into the cash-box of the First Consul. But Bourrienne's hands were not clean in money matters, and that was an unpardonable sin in anyone who desired to be in real intimacy with Napoleon. He became involved in the affairs of the House of Coulon, which failed, and in October, 1802, he was called on to hand over his office. After Napoleon's fall he sided with the Bourbons and was made minister of state without portfolio by King Louis XVIII. The ruin of his finances drove him out of France, but he eventually died in a madhouse at Caen.

When his book *Memoirs of Napoleon Bonaparte* first appeared in 1829, it made a sensation. Until then in most writings Napoleon had been treated as either a demon or a demi-god. The real facts of the case were not suited to the tastes of either his enemies or his admirers.

Shmuel Moreh, professor of Arabic language and literature at Hebrew University in Jerusalem, is editor of the *Literary Magazine in Arabic* on Israeli TV. He is the author and editor of ten books including *Modern Arabic Poetry 1800–1970: The Development of its Forms and Themes under the Influence of Western Literature, Studies in Modern Arabic Prose and Poetry,* and *Live Theatre and Dramatic Literature in the Medieval Arab World* and numerous articles.

EDWARD W. SAID, professor of English and comparative literature at Columbia University, is author of numerous books, including *Beginnings: Intention and Method, Covering Islam, The World, the Text and the Critic,* and *Culture and Imperialism,* and numerous articles.

ROBERT L. TIGNOR, professor of history at Princeton University, is an associate editor of *World Politics* and member of the editorial board of the *International Journal of Middle Eastern Studies.* He is the author of five books, including *Egypt and Sudan, The Colonial Transformation of Kenya: The Kamba, Kikuyu & Maasai from 1900–1939* and *State, Private Enterprise and Economic Change in Egypt, 1918–1952* and numerous articles.

Endnotes: to Al-Jabartī:

[1]The first date represents the Muslim calendar, the second the Western, Gregorian one.

[2]Its autograph (handwritten manuscript by the author) is in the Leiden University library.

[3]The autograph of this book is in the Cambridge University Library.

[4]The autograph is in the Cambridge University Library.

[5]No autograph of this has been discovered. According to Jurî Zaydan there is a manuscript in the library of Muḥammad Bek Āṣif in Cairo, copied by Aḥmad b. Ḥasan al-Rashīdī in 1237/1821, and revised by al-Jabartī on November 6, 1824 (see *Tārīkh Ādāb al-Lugha al-'Arabiyya,* IV, 283, cf. D. Ayalon, *BSOAS,* XXII, Pt. 2 (1960), 229, n. 3).

[6]Translated by D. Crelecius and 'Abd al-Wahhāb Bakr (Leiden, E.J. Brill, 1992).

[7]See S. Moreh, *Al-Jabartī's Chronicle. . . . ,* p. 47.

[8]See al-Sharqāwī, *Miṣr fī 'l-Qarn al-Thāmin 'Aṣhar* (Cairo, 1955), 1, 15–16.

Bibliography

A. 'l. 'Abd al-Karīm (ed.), *'Abd al-Raḥmān al-Jabartī: Dirāsāt wa-Buḥūth* (Cairo, 1976); David Ayalon, "The Historian al-Jabartī and His Background," *BSOAS,* xxiii, pt. 2 (1960), 217–49; David Ayalon, *'al-Jabarti,* in *E.l.* 2; Brockelmann, *GAL,* Suppl. 11, 731; 'Adil Manna', 'Cultural Relations between Egyptian and Jerusalem 'Ulama' in the Early Nineteenth Century', *Asian and African Studies,* Haifa, XVII, nos. 1–2, 1983, 139–152; Shmuel Moreh, *Al-Jabartī's Chronicle of the First Seven Months of the French Occupation of Egypt,* ed. and trans. S. Moreh (Leiden, 1975); M. al-Sharqāwī, *Dirāsāt fī Tārīkh al-Jabartī, Miṣr fi 'l-Qarn al-Thāmin' Ashar* (Cairo, 1955–56), 3 Vols,; Kh. Shaybūb, *'Abd al-Raḥmān al-Jabartī* (Cairo, 1948); J.-D. al-Sheyyāl, *A History of Egyptian Historiography in the Nineteenth Century* (Alexandria, 1958).